I0085588

DISCUSSION AT A MONASTERY

Discussion at a Monastery

✠ ✠ ✠

By Monk Macarius

(of the Holy Monastery of the Dormition of the Theotokos, Penteli, Attica, Greece)

Translated and edited by Lawrence Damian Robinson

Ἐπίγνωσις

EPIGNOSIS PUBLISHING

Discussion at a Monastery
Copyright © 2014 by Lawrence Damian Robinson

All rights reserved. No part of this book may be copied, reproduced or distributed in any form, whether in print or by any audio, visual, electronic or mechanical means, including through information storage and retrieval systems, without the express written permission of the publisher or the publisher's legally authorized agent. An exception to the foregoing prohibition is granted to reviewers, who may quote brief passages from this book in a review.

Epignosis Publishing
P.O. Box 682
Princeton, NJ 08542-0682

The Epignosis Publishing name and logo are trademarks of Epignosis Publishing in the United States of America. For rights inquiries, contact: publisher@epignosispublishing.com.

First edition: March 2014
20 19 18 17 16 15 14 13 12 11   1 2 3 4 5
ISBN: 978-0-6159867-3-9

DISCUSSION AT A MONASTERY

Translator's Foreword

One of the truly marvelous things about living in an Orthodox country such as Greece is the incredible number of spiritual 'centers' of which one can avail oneself. They are seemingly everywhere, and one can take advantage of their spiritual wealth without a great deal of effort or sacrifice. These 'centers' are places of refreshment, places of rest, and places of healing—like oases in the desert of life—where one can obtain a drink of vivifying and fortifying water, before continuing on one's hard journey through the wilderness. They are the monasteries.

These life-giving oases are so important, and yet they are so often taken for granted or even misunderstood. For this reason, a little book like *Discussion at a Monastery*, is such a welcome addition to the growing body of contemporary Orthodox spiritual literature now available in English.

In simple language, the author, writing from his own experience as a monk, and from that of others whom he has encountered on his spiritual journey, describes the meaning of the monastic life—a Christ-centered life that is first and foremost about self-examination and prayer. But this book is not only for monastics. In its pages there are many deep truths about the purpose of the spiritual life that will challenge any reader, layperson or monk, to take a closer look at his or her own life of prayer—which is to say, his or her own relationship with God.

I had the great honor and privilege of translating this little book after meeting Monk Macarius in person for the first time shortly after Christmas of 2012. I had seen him many times at the local monastery where I usually attended services—a small, wizened-looking, older monk who tended to stay to himself and to leave quickly after the services. But something about his presence and the intensity of his prayerful concentration—whether during Vespers or Matins or Divine Liturgy—impressed me, and on more than one occasion I found myself wondering who this monk was.

One day, as I was leaving the church after some service or other, I saw Monk Macarius, who had left a little before me, standing outside waiting. I was pleasantly surprised when he called me over and asked to have a word with me. He handed me a small book as a gift, and said that he would be grateful to hear my opinion about it, if I had a chance to read it.

That book, *Discussion at a Monastery* (*Συζήτηση Σε Μοναστήρι* in Greek), impressed me so much as I began to read it that I decided that it had to be translated, in order that those who were unable to read it in its original Greek could reap the benefits of the wisdom it contained. I hope that other readers will find it as inspiring and as spiritually edifying as I did.

—*Lawrence Damian Robinson*
Penteli, Athens, Greece
February, 2014

Prologue

The questions I received from many acquaintances of mine, as well as from people I did not know, gave me an excuse to present this book. All of the questions referred to here were put to me by people who were looking for an answer to their queries. The events to which I refer are real.

I thank everyone who would have the kindness to make known to me their opinion about the text that follows.

—*Monk Macarius*
Athens, 2001

Vespers had finished. Then, out of the compunction of our prayers, my friends and I went out into the courtyard of the monastery. We sat and enjoyed the sunset, which had slowly begun to cast its shadows around us. At some point, a monk heading towards some chapel passed close beside us. Our friend, Timon, greeted him and asked him to stay and talk to us. The monk, Fr. Theopistus, agreed and Timon asked him:

TIMON: We see a lot of monks in your monastery, Father, most of whom are young. Are all of these monks true to what they have chosen to follow? Do they all live a higher spiritual life?

THEOPISTUS: The monks who live a higher spiritual life are few. Most of us inside the monastery find ourselves at the stage of making an effort, of learning, and we can't yet say that we are at a high spiritual level.

TIMON: Father, your answer makes an impression on me. I expressed that question of mine because a friend of mine returned a few days ago from the monastery where his son is a novice monk, and he was not very pleased with the discussion he had with some of the monastics there. My friend formed the opinion that those monks, from what they were saying, showed spiritual immaturity and an unclear knowledge of monasticism. One of the monks he spoke with was a doctor and another one was a theologian. My friend was not satisfied even with them. He is wondering if his son is going to be happy living in that monastery.

THEOPISTUS: Whoever wants to become a monk, if he understands what monasticism is, knows how to achieve his goal: he takes care of himself. Others' imperfections don't affect him. He only sees his target. But you talked about the spiritual life. What do you mean by that term?

TIMON: Many activities could be characterized as the spiritual life. For monks, that would be the study of books. You, Father, what would you call the spiritual life?

THEOPISTUS: We consider the spiritual life to be related to the sciences and the arts. I think that, to be precise, we should not call these manifestations the spiritual life, but a concept and an art, because they are energies of the brain and of the emotions.

Whatever is related to truth, to righteousness, and to discernment belongs to the spirit. Our spirit has to have some special quality for us to want to accept the truth, for us to give righteousness its practical meaning. For us to have a spiritual life, our spirit would have to find itself in its natural condition—to be healthy.

Our logic and our feelings turn us away from our spirit. Intellectuals and artists might be spiritual people, or they might not be. The same is true for those who are illiterate, as well as for those who are not occupied with the arts.

The spiritual life is the experiences of virtuous people, those who have become like Christ wants us to be. Spirituality has nothing to do with knowledge.

TIMON: Do monks find the conditions that will help them progress in the spiritual life inside a monastery?

THEOPISTUS: Yes. They have the guidance of the abbot, assuming of course that the abbot is himself a true monk. They also have their hours for prayer, as well as the writings of the Holy Fathers of the Church. In the monastery there are also those real monks, the virtuous ones, the few, who are usually unseen, unknown to the crowds, because they don't want to put themselves on display. They also become an example for the others.

TIMON: The monks that haven't progressed spiritually— can we characterize them as neglectful and even unreliable? In that case, what meaning does their stay in the monastery have?

THEOPISTUS: Monasteries are also schools and doctor's offices. For many monastics, it takes a long time to be able to get into step with the rules of the monastery. Those rules are aimed first and foremost at the deliverance of the man from his defects, from his passions. This task is difficult, laborious, but that's what it is to be a monk. "It's hard being a monk."

Monks with polite, impeccable outward behavior can be unreliable if they don't work on their spiritual progress. For those monks, who can't catch hold of the spirit of monasticism, it is not pleasant to be isolated and to keep themselves under control—something that means that they are not able to pray.

It requires some strength for us to be able to live only with ourselves without our souls becoming filled with boredom. It requires us, when we are alone, to want to turn towards God. Then we'll be able to stand ourselves and we will try to be true to what we have chosen.

The monastery keeps even those who have a hard time progressing in the spiritual life to give them the possibility of uncovering, sooner or later, the purpose of the monastic life.

We monks who have not progressed spiritually find ourselves in different situations. Some of us, conformed to the spirit of monasticism and making an effort to be healed of our passions, are trying to maintain the correct attitude towards God. Others of us again are not yet able to become conscious of our imperfections, and because of that our attitude towards God is not a fitting one. That has the consequence that our bad spiritual condition remains static or that, within the monastery, we even become worse.

TIMON: Those who don't manage to comply with the monastic rules—didn't they understand the difficulty before becoming monks?

THEOPISTUS: Most of us decided to become monks without knowing the purpose of monasticism. We have insufficient and incorrect knowledge, or total ignorance of the methods of the monastic life. That ignorance explains our difficult course as monks. During our trial period as novices, we weren't able to become aware of the meaning of our choice, maybe also because of the inadequacy of the abbot.

This situation inside the monasteries shouldn't surprise us, because it is the same as the situation of people in the wider community. It's just that our way of expressing our imperfections is not the same as everyone else's. Do you believe that outside of the monasteries you will find many perfect people?

Diogenes, in order to show how difficult it is for us to be perfect, went around at noon with a lighted lamp, seeking to find a real person. The philosopher recognized that we who appear normal, smiling, of good disposition, polite, have something hidden inside us that, with a trivial excuse, can show its ugliness.

Diogenes circled around whomever did not have that repugnant thing inside him. We monastics come out of that society and bring its image into the monasteries, our faults, which we don't even suspect. The few real monks put their own element into that picture, just like the few exceptional people give their own inspiration outside the monastery.

TIMON: I think that monks don't come out of that wider society, but rather out of those circles with in it that have some special relationship with the Church. That's why people see— want to see—the monastics as people with high spirituality.

THEOPISTUS: Among the monks there are also those who, before coming to monasticism, lived in a way that had nothing to do with the spirit of the Church. They changed a little before deciding to become monks. I know some of those who consciously live in accordance with the rules of monasticism.

Of those who had lengthy sojourns in the bosom of the Church before coming to monasticism, it seems that they have not absorbed all of the meaning of the teachings of the Gospel. Most know whatever they heard in the Sunday Schools or in religious organizations. Apart from some exceptions, people (whether clerics or laypeople) who learned the teachings of the Church intellectually or professionally at the university taught them. The education, as well as the spirituality, of those people is based more or less on the writings of some non-Orthodox foreigners rather than on the works of the Fathers of our Church.

We can't be brought into personal communion with God, nor can we know Him, with knowledge that is acquired. But Christ tells us that our eternal life is to know Him. The knowledge of God, of Christ, gives life to our souls.

Christ does not want us to be spiritual vegetables. He wants our spirit to be so clear, so alive, as to be able to see and to know Him. In the Gospel, we read His words: *"And this is eternal life, that they may know You, the only true God, and Jesus Christ whom You have sent."* (John 17:3) The lessons that we study will have meaning if we learn how to know God.

We learn different things about God with our mind, but we can't know God Himself. We know God if our spirit is pure. *"Blessed are the pure in heart, for they shall see God."* (Mt 5:8) Our spirit becomes pure through prayer.

Philosophy, the other sciences, and art have their value, of course. However, they can't absolutely fulfill the requirements of our soul. Naturally they can't lead us to the knowledge of God. Books with the teaching of our Church Fathers enter into the understanding of the words of our Christ, and I will tell you now about the lovely surprise that I experienced when some people showed me their appreciation for one of those books, the *Philokalia*[1].

---

[1] The *Philokalia* is a collection of writings from various monastic Saints of the Church, and particularly of those desert Saints who practiced *hesychia* (stillness) and *nepsis* (watchfulness). The texts, whose dates of authorship range from the fourth through roughly the fifteenth centuries, were compiled in the eighteenth century by St. Nicodemus of the Holy Mountain (Athos) and St. Macarius of Corinth. A major theme of the compilation is 'spiritual warfare', and it is considered one of the classics of Orthodox Christian spiritual literature.—*Trans.*

A young man—a student at a technical school—who was unknown to me until that moment, wanted to have a talk with me. During the course of the conversation, I suggested that we read something from the *Philokalia*, a book that was unknown to him. He requested that we analyze the excerpt that I had read at random. The next time he visited me, he told me that he had bought that book, the *Philokalia*, which we know is very difficult.

Someone else who met me by chance in the monastery's courtyard—someone I didn't know—stood there and said to me: "Father, a short time ago I found out about the *Philokalia*. I didn't know that we had those kinds of treasures." I asked him what he did for a living. He replied that he was a chauffeur and a truck driver. He was about forty years old.

A woman acquaintance of mine, an architect, said to me about the same book that she had dedicated an entire year to studying each of its five volumes. Another female acquaintance of mine, an Italian doctor, systematically enjoyed another book, *Saint Symeon the New Theologian*. I don't know if there are many of us who, when we went to become monks, knew of the existence of these books.

TIMON: People who decide to become monks without having grasped the meaning of monasticism—what's their motive for making that choice?

THEOPISTUS: For some of us, the motive is a rudimentary devoutness. Others, based on the enthusiastic words of some cassock-wearers, consider the monastic life to be easy and decide to become monks, believing that in that way we become important. And there are also those of us who believe that we are perfect (without knowing what perfection is). Because of that, we consider ourselves chosen by God and we come to monasticism in order to do God the favor of dedicating our "perfection" to Him.

But for someone to become a true monk (which is to say, a true person), he has to come to the monastery with an appreciation of his imperfections and with the desire to have a teacher. Only those that have the correct faith in God do that.

TIMON: Father, you must have some specific cases among your fellow monks, from which what you are referring to can be seen.

THEOPISTUS: Yes. A certain monk who had been living for five years in the monastery said to me: "I came to be a monk so that I could become a Saint. Now I'm beginning to realize what I have to do in order to accomplish that." That man had left his job abroad to become a monk.

In another conversation with a monk I know, I referred to an event from the life of the first years of monasticism, as follows: An ascetic hermit, famed for his virtue, visited a large monastery with many monks for a few days. The day he left there for his place of asceticism, they asked him his opinion about the life of the monks of that monastery. He said that he wasn't certain that many of those monks would save their souls.

My interlocutor was unhappy with what he heard and said to me: "Is it possible for us monks not to save our souls? I thought that all we monks were going to heaven. You disappoint me." A little earlier, he was criticizing some monks to me, saying that they weren't performing their duties properly. He believed, in short, that it was enough for someone to wear the cassock in order to be God's elect. That man had spent twenty years in the monastic life.

Other monastics show their relationship to monasticism by declaring that they are having a nice time in their monastery. I accidentally heard a young monk at some monastery saying to lay visitors: "I'm confused, because the old monks wish us 'good patience'. But we're having such a good time!"

Such was that monk's knowledge about monasticism, that he didn't understand the meaning of the blessing, "good patience". And to think that Christ Himself recommends patience to us. He tells us that with our patience we will heal our souls. *"In your patience win your souls."* (Lk 21:19)

The "good", for monks, is connected with the spiritual life. How did that young monk manage in a short time to achieve such spirituality that he was having a good time? In order to do the will of God, the holy ascetics undertook hard trials upon themselves. And even the Apostle Paul, who ascended into Heaven and heard "unspeakable words", was given a "thorn in the flesh"—a bodily illness that tormented him (2 Cor. 12:7)—so that he wouldn't have such a good time and would be able to maintain his balance.

Likewise, patience is needed to pass through the narrow gate about which Christ speaks to us: *"Strive to enter in through the narrow gate...."* (Lk 13:24) Here I also remember the answer that a metropolitan I know gave when he was asked how he was doing. "It's like I find myself on a cross," he said. Seeing our confusion, he explained to us that his contact with the dramas of people—family troubles and such—made him sad.

We discover the ignorance that many of us have about the purpose of monasticism on the same day that we become monks. While we are being tonsured, at the exact moment that we declare, inside the church, our desire to follow the monastic life, the chanters chant the following *troparion*:

"Hasten to open a fatherly embrace to me, who have consumed my life as a prodigal. In the inexhaustible wealth of your mercies Savior, do not now overlook an impoverished heart. To you, Lord, do I cry out in compunction, I have sinned, save me!"

With this prayer, we appeal to God, and we confess to Him our decision to dedicate ourselves to the perfect knowledge and performance of His will, and we beseech him to accept us and to keep us near Him, in His embrace.

I was speaking once with an acquaintance of mine the day after his tonsure. I made a point of the importance of that *troparion*. He told me that he didn't know it. When it was being chanted at the time of his tonsure, he didn't notice it—his mind was somewhere else. From this it can be understood that, at that moment, he's the one who should have said that *troparion*. I suppose that he was praying to God at that moment.

Now, through our discussion, he was given an opportunity to learn about that *troparion*. But it seemed that he couldn't understand the meaning of the hymn; he saw that it wasn't in harmony with the "world" of his soul. After a while another monk showed, at the time we were speaking, that he was also a stranger to the meaning of that *troparion*.

From the conduct of most monks, it becomes obvious that the only thing we don't pursue is our march towards God's embrace. Maybe because we believe we have already found it. In that case, we mean "God's embrace" in the way that we want.

How many of us believe that we have consumed our life prodigally? Why, we went to Sunday School, we attended homilies and Bible studies, we went to church regularly.... Can the sovereignty of egotism over us be considered as prodigality? It's incomprehensible. But whoever appeals to God conscientiously with the *troparion* that I referred to, accepts that his heart is "impoverished"—that is to say, poor in the virtues. Most of us show that we don't agree at all with that point of the *troparion*.

During their tonsure, some allow their tears to run. And they give the impression of being conscientious monks. Very soon however—even a little while after their tonsure—they prove that their tears were not tears of compunction, but tears of emotion. But emotion is a situation that has nothing to do with the meaning of our tonsure. Even our tears sometimes show our ignorance about the meaning of monasticism.

Anyway, that *troparion*, which is there for a reason, will continue to be chanted every time there is a monastic tonsure.

TIMON: Since monasteries are places of healing, what therapeutic methods do they apply?

THEOPISTUS: Naturally monasteries are places of spiritual healing. For the treatment of the soul we have teaching, confession, as well as some exercises, some tests. A basic rule for the spiritual progress of monks is confession—reporting to the abbot all of the problems, all of the thoughts that occupy them. With that confession, the monks free themselves from the questions that preoccupy them and they apply themselves undistractedly to prayer.

I won't refer to trials that we read about in different books, like the *Ladder of Divine Ascent* of Saint John of Sinai. I'll tell you about the test that an abbot I know put to a novice monk, when I had visited him at his monastery. At that time the mother of the abbot happened to be there. The abbot, in front of his mother and me, as a test, said to the novice:

THE ABBOT:	*Why don't you watch where you're going, you ass?*
THE MOTHER:	*Don't call the boy an ass.*
THE ABBOT:	*But he is one!*
THE MOTHER:	*Well, don't remind him of it...*

At the last words of the mother, whose intervention we didn't expect, we remained speechless for some seconds, and then, along with the novice, we broke out into convulsive laughter—all except for the mother. She, understanding what she had said, smiled with a characteristic air.

At that time only the abbot and the novice were living in the monastery. Today the former novice is a monk and, besides him, another three young monks are living there. Such tests happen in order for us to become aware of the degree of our egotism.

TIMON: Father, you said that some in the monastery can get worse. I can't understand that.

THEOPISTUS: The ones who want to seem important out of egotism get worse. They form such an unrealistic image for themselves that they lose their personality and they even arrive at insanity. They feed themselves the fantasy that they have all the virtues of the perfect monk—that they are Saints. They despise the others.

In our monastery, a few years ago, there lived a monk who believed that he was perfect. Praying in his cell more than what the abbot had stipulated, he compared himself to the other monks and he found them beneath him. He learned at some point that a monk from our monastery, when he went to some city on duty, ate meat—something that was forbidden by the canons. He condemned that monk and boasted that he would never eat meat.

One day he appeared in the courtyard entirely naked, and he stood there and sang. His face was wild—he had been possessed. The monastery sent him to a neurological clinic. After a while his situation was considered to have improved and they brought him to the monastery. When he sat at the table to eat with us, he put the food in his mouth and immediately he spat it out, spraying it right and left. He had been sitting across from me.

Egotism made that monk boast of virtues that he didn't have, but he thought he had. However egotism also harms us when we feed it with abilities that we really have. An acquaintance of mine, a layman, had a stellar record in the science that he had studied. He has been dealing with psychological problems for a long time. His spiritual situation isn't good. He resorted to a psychiatrist. When we talked, I spoke to him about contempt for others, into which egotism impels us. He looked at me surprised and said: "That's what I do. I see others as beneath me and I despise them...."

TIMON: How can monks who remain spiritually stagnant be satisfied with their lives?

THEOPISTUS: Some of us are satisfied and peaceful because we believe we are good with God only because we wear a cassock and live in a monastery. That makes us consider ourselves as important and exceptional personalities, worthy of accepting the pilgrimages of pious Christians. That is a sort of satisfaction for us.

Others, to give some kind of meaning to our lives, do intellectual work: we write books or give speeches. Of course that kind of work is good. When, however, we perform it without experiencing and without applying the beautiful things that we write and say, we don't gain anything.

There are also those who "fill" their lives taking care of the salvation of the souls of others, believing that they have ensured their own salvation. They don't miss an opportunity to "teach" monks and laypeople, even uninvited. In such a way, they come out of obscurity (which others seek) and gain the reputation of the good monk. That pleases them.

Others pursue taking over a position of leadership in the monastery and give meaning to their lives when they achieve it. Of course, those substitutes for monasticism superficially hide the emptiness of our souls. Some others manage to look deeper and then they discover another world.

II

TIMON: Those who are true monks—what motive led them to monasticism?

THEOPISTUS: The real monk decides to live the monastic life motivated by his love for Christ.

Of those who conscientiously become monks, from love for Christ, some have the weight of sin in their souls. They see that their souls are sick. They seek healing, and they understand that they will need a lot of time to find their soul's health. They understand that the only one who can heal them, and who wants to heal them, is Christ. That's why they love Him.

They repent of their sins. Their repentance leads them to a place from which they are undistractedly occupied with the healing of their soul—it leads them to the monastery. There they mourn, for they are sick, and they beseech Christ, the doctor whom they love, to give their souls comfort.

They know that Christ loves them because they hear His words, those that are written in the Gospel: Come to me, you who are loaded with the weight of sin and exhausted, you who have been disappointed seeking your happiness far away from me; come, I will give you rest. *"Come to Me, all you who labor and are burdened, and I will give you rest."* (Mt 11:28)

Others may not have the heavy burden of sin in their souls, but they see their imperfections and their difficulty in becoming perfect—in becoming the way God wants them to be. They take note of the obstacles that exist within their souls and around them. In order to be freed of those obstacles that make their spiritual life difficult, they too are led to the monastery. There they can have the means of doing the will of Christ. They can have, as much as it is possible, more time to allow their souls to seek Christ through prayer.

Surely others who don't want to become monks love Christ, too. They are able to live according to the will of God in the cities and to reach the height of perfection, just like monks.

Saint Anthony wanted to learn how much he had advanced in virtue. In Alexandria there lived a shoe repairman—a cobbler. God suggested to Saint Anthony to visit that cobbler and to compare himself with him. Saint Anthony went to become acquainted with the spirituality of a layperson, not of a monk. He got a lesson about his spiritual journey from a layman, even though other ascetic monks lived near him.

Saint Anthony spoke with the cobbler. He learned that he practiced guarding himself against egotism and that he was a bearer of humility. For that reason, he thought daily that all people were good and that only he was a sinner.

Saint Anthony understood that the cobbler had found the way by which a person reaches perfection in the spiritual life and becomes the way God wants us to be. He decided to imitate the cobbler. When he met with his fellow ascetics, Anthony told them about the asceticism the cobbler practiced. They said that that kind of asceticism was too difficult for them. And they were monks!

TIMON: How do the ascetics who live on their own manage not to be afflicted with boredom in their solitude?

THEOPISTUS: I'm perplexed by that, too. I visited some monks who live by themselves and I wanted to know what their lives were like, because I was also thinking about trying to live alone.

I saw that two of the ones I met spent their days occupied with their handicrafts and their gardens. They dedicated little time to prayer. They read vespers and matins more out of convention. They seemed pleased with their lives. Their giving themselves over to those deeds, the external ones, made them not suffer boredom in their solitude—or rather not to be aware of their boredom, because I have a hard time believing that a person who has so much time for prayer at his disposal can pray so little and not have an emptiness inside.

Those people must not get it, that the satisfaction that life of theirs gives them is superficial. I think that the way in which those monks live is not the normal monastic life. They live, or so it seems, like most other people who, absorbed with different pursuits, don't turn their attention towards the state of their inner selves. They aren't interested in learning how far away they are from the pinnacle of perfection.

Our mind, which has so many capabilities, is unable to recognize who we are, and how we should be. Our spirit, when it is not healthy, darkens our mind and leads it to mistaken activities. Our spirit has to be healthy for our mind to work properly.

The life of another hermit I met was different from the life of those two whom I mentioned before. From the conversations that I had with him, I understood that he wanted to do the will of God, and to become like Christ tells us to be. For that reason, he practices watchfulness ('*nepsis*')—paying attention to himself. He takes care not to allow his mind to become preoccupied with fruitless thoughts, which can impede him from being directed towards God and from praying within his heart.

That ascetic is free from boredom, not because he is entertained by different pursuits, but because through his prayer he has peace and quietude ('*hesychia*') in his soul. Because he sees that he is not alone. He sees that God, towards Whom he directs himself, loves him and wants to give him true joy.

At the beginning of his ascetic life, that ascetic saw his mind ('*nous*') make a motion to cast out boredom, as if it pushed it to go out from him. At the same time he believed that, in place of boredom, it would certainly bring him comfort. He noted with terror that instead of comfort, he saw turmoil inside himself. Luckily he was saved from that situation, because he succeeded in saying a few words of prayer. Otherwise, as he told me, he would have fallen into despair.

Now, in the depths of his heart, sorrow and grief appear to him, together with tranquility. He understood that in the situation in which his soul found itself, it could only mourn. It wasn't possible for him to know joy yet. He became aware that in order to be able to have joy, his soul had to be healed from its vices, from its passions—and that until he accomplished that, naturally it had to grieve.

He began to practice mourning. He understood that he had to do the opposite of what he had done at the beginning. Not to look for joy, but to look for sorrow. Something upside down, anyone would say. A sick situation, someone else might say, judging offhandedly. The ascetic now practices having his soul immersed in grief and directing it towards the depths of his heart. And from that depth, to ask Christ for His mercy.

Achieving that is based on self-knowledge. He brings to his mind the reasons for his mourning, and he has his imperfections before him. His prayer finds a firm foundation on top of his mourning—prayer that will at some point cast the grief out of his soul and will lead him to the knowledge of the true joy that is now unknown to him. However, steadfastness and security—which, as he says, the perception of reality and the knowledge of the truth give him—are known to him.

TIMON: The hermit, as you tell us, Father, is fine, even though he lives alone. He's fine because, inside his soul, he finds reasons that give him comfort. We have the possibility of listening to some "Kalamatian"[2], or some "triple" concert, or to Joan Baez. We even watch some side-splitting comedy. We enjoy a conversation over drinks with friends. If we want to, we go skiing. The desert-dweller doesn't enjoy any of that, or any other pleasures. He doesn't even have a companion to converse with. I'm having a hard time, despite everything you told us, understanding how it's possible for him not to ever have some kind of sadness in his solitude.

THEOPISTUS: Not all hermits succeed in being free from sorrow right from the beginning of their ascetic life. Many of them have anxiety, even when they are praying, because they haven't been healed of their egotism. They find their soul's rest little by little.

Even when they have fully progressed in the spiritual life and can have the peace of prayer, many times desert-dwellers have experienced intense sorrow. The chirping of a bird or the beauty of a flower happens to have been able to cast out their

---

[2] This is a reference to the music accompanying a traditional dance from Kalamata in the southern part of the Peloponnese peninsula. —*Trans.*

grief. But even monks who live in monasteries and find themselves in daily contact with many people have a hard time putting up with the limitations of the rules of monastic life.

A monk I know was telling me that when the time came for us to shut ourselves up in our cells, such as after Compline, he would go to his cell, but he couldn't stay there. He didn't feel like reading any books. He couldn't pray. He would go out of his cell to find someone to talk to, or he would sit alone on a balcony daydreaming until it was time for bed. Such cases also show that many of us come to live as monks unprepared. Finally, after many years, my monk acquaintance managed to be able to comply with the rules of monasticism.

We know that Saint Anthony understood how it's not easy for everyone to have their *nous* constantly attached to the hard work of prayer. That's why he allowed his disciples to occupy themselves with games too. The following event is well-known:

Some passerby, coming upon the place where the disciples of Saint Anthony were living as monks, saw them playing, shooting arrows at a target with a bow. He said to Saint Anthony that it wasn't fitting for monks to play, nor could he understand that monks also had need of rest. Because of that, Saint Anthony gave him a bow and told him to stretch out its string.

When the passerby had done that, Saint Anthony told him to stretch out the string further. He answered that if he stretched the string further, it would break. Then Saint Anthony said to him: And if the monks occupy themselves with their spiritual work without a break, they won't be able to stand the fatigue that work brings about, just like the bowstring can't withstand being stretched beyond a certain limit.

Christ likens the kingdom of the heavens to a treasure, which we find hidden in a field, and in our joy we sell everything we have to buy that field. (Mt 13:44) The field in which the treasure is found is our soul. The desert-dwelling monk succeeds in enduring loneliness and the laborious spiritual struggle, because through his asceticism he has uncovered precious treasure in the depths of his heart—the peace of the kingdom of God. The more an ascetic progresses in spirituality, the more easily he faces loneliness.

TIMON: We Christians have to do the will of God. How do monks do the will of God inside the monastery?

THEOPISTUS: To answer that question, we have to understand what the will of God is. Christ tells us that the will of God is for us to become perfect. *"You shall be perfect, even as your Father Who is in the heavens is perfect."* (Mt 5:48) If monks try to become perfect people, they are doing the will of God.

TIMON: Yes, but with what kind of work do monks become perfect?

THEOPISTUS: The work with which we all become perfect is accomplished inside of us, in our spirit; it is invisible, hidden in the depths of each one of us. Only God knows it. For that work of theirs, Christians seek the advice of their spiritual father. Monks dedicate a lot of time to that work and they perform it with the instructions of their abbot.

Of course, that invisible work which belongs to our souls beautifies our external behavior as well, and reveals itself through the energies of our essence. That work is prayer. The tasks that invisibly, mystically, lead us into perfection are accomplished in our hearts and in our spirits through prayer.

III

TIMON: How does a person become perfect through prayer?

THEOPISTUS: The spiritually healthy person is perfect—he who has his soul in a natural condition, which is the way Christ wants us. By ourselves, we cannot become perfect. God gives us perfection. When we live in accordance with His commandments, when our soul is like He tells us, we are perfect.

Christ tells us that without Him we can do nothing: *"...without me you are not able to do anything."* (John 15:5) To be sure, people who don't believe in Christ do important work. But they are unable to accomplish the most important work—their own perfection. When Christ tells us "without me you are not able to do anything", he is referring to exactly that which we must do in order to become perfect.

Even without believing in Christ, our mind can function. But for all the powers of our soul and our spirit to be in a natural state, we have to want to accept Christ. This volition of ours is expressed by prayer. With prayer we seek out Christ. We don't seek perfection—we seek the Perfect One. Perfection doesn't give us comfort—the Perfect One comforts us.

Without the Perfect One, there is no perfection. Perfection is not something that exists autonomously and that we can acquire whenever we want, nor is it an abstract concept. Perfection is understood only as something recognizable, as the attribute of a person—of that person above whom there is no other person; of that person whose power is within himself[3]. That person is God—is Christ.

God is perfect, because He does not receive His perfection from someone else. His perfection does not change. We acquire perfection progressively. To be sure, we can't be absolutely perfect, like God. If we stop being in communion with Christ, we lose our perfection. Our Christ asks that we become perfect. That is, that we develop our spiritual abilities to the highest point that our nature is capable of.

If our capacity is limited to the perception of nature's perfection, we are incomplete, underdeveloped. Our perfection reaches its summit when we can see—when we can know—the Perfect One, God. Of course we can't know the essence of God. We know God's energies.

Christ makes those who love Him perfect, because he gives them His gifts. When we receive the gifts of Christ, we have the experience of perfection, because whatever Christ gives us is something from Himself. He gives us His own peace and His

---

[3] Literally "of that person who is 'self-powered'". —*Trans.*

own joy. He tells us that Himself: *"Peace I leave to you, <u>My</u> peace I give to you..."* (John 14:27), and, *"These things I have spoken to you, that <u>My</u> joy might remain in you, and that your joy might be made full."* (John 15:11) "<u>My own</u> peace I give to you," and I want "<u>My own</u> joy to remain in your souls."

What is the peace of Christ like? The Apostle Paul tells us that it is so excellent that the mind of man cannot understand its perfection: *"And the peace of God, which surpasses all understanding, will guard your hearts...."* (Php. 4:7)

If a man wants to become perfect with the goal of admiring himself, he doesn't achieve anything, because he is trying to deify himself. If we don't know Christ, we can't know what it is that we call perfection. Who can say what the perfect man is like? Our Christ tells us to become perfect, because our heavenly father is perfect. *"You shall be perfect, even as your Father Who is in the heavens is perfect."* (Mt 5:48)

Regarding the absoluteness of the perfection of God, I remember a discussion I had with a Marxist—a relative of mine. He wanted to tell me that the faith of the Christians was incorrect. He considered it a mistake of ours that we believed in the absolute, while—in his opinion— there was no such thing as the absolute. I answered him that even he believed in the absolute, because if he accepted that Marxist theory was not absolutely correct, he accepted that it was incorrect, at least in some of its points. When he heard that, he was displeased and changed the subject of the conversation.

To become perfect, we have to ask of Christ to make Himself known to us. When we know God, we don't want to pay attention to our own perfection. We understand that the object of our perfection is the vision of God. We become perfect in order to be able to see God. Admiration of our own perfection doesn't give us our satisfaction, our blessedness. Our blessedness, our joy, is the vision of the beauty of the Perfect One—of Christ.

In order to be able to know God, our heart has to become pure, and our heart becomes pure through prayer.

TIMON:　　　Are you trying to say, Father, that with the prayers that we make in church, we all become perfect?

THEOPISTUS:　The time that we have at our disposal for prayer in church is not sufficient to help us become perfect. Those who become aware of the need for prayer, pray spontaneously and at times when they are not in church. For that reason they close themselves in their rooms—in their "*chamber*" (Mt 6:6)— for prayer.

Besides that, inside the church it is difficult to concentrate on ourselves. The many prayer books, the melodies of the hymns, our movements inside the church, all disrupt our attention from the meaning of prayer. For that reason, few manage to pray perfectly there. Those few can become perfect, although certainly they also pray when they are not inside the church.

Prayer is the most important act of the Christian. During the Divine Liturgy, we prepare to receive Holy Communion with prayer. However, if we do not commune noetically with Christ when we pray, we cannot say that we commune with Him when we accept Holy Communion. We keep the gifts of Holy Communion in our souls with prayer.

With prayer, we are attentive to the depths of our soul and we keep watch over its functioning. We become aware of our failings and our passions. We have right reasoning and clear understanding, and an enlightened mind (*nous*). We acquire the virtues. We accept and hold in the depths of our heart the peace of Christ.

The prayer that leads us to the height of perfection is the expression of our will to have Christ in our heart. We beseech our Christ to make us worthy to see Him, and we know that He wants to be present, to appear to us. He Himself tells us: I love him who loves me and I will appear to him. We read His words in the Gospel: *"He who has My commandments and keeps them, it is he who loves Me. And he who loves Me will be loved by My Father, and I will love him and <u>manifest Myself to him</u>."* (John 14:21)

We seek Christ out with our prayer, because we hear Him say that He wants to have us as friends—for us to remain united with Him and for Him to remain united with us: *"You are My friends if you do whatever I command you"* (John 15:14) and *"abide in Me, and I in you."* (John 15:4) But while we seek Christ, when we see that our heart is not straightened up and clean, so as to be able to see Him, we are saddened and we mourn. With our prayer, we ask him to purify our heart in order for it to become a place that is ready for us to receive Him there.

Through prayer we gather into the depths of our heart the powers of our *nous* that have been scattered outside of us, and we become well-formed personalities. The words of our prayer, hidden in the depths of our heart like yeast inside of a lot of dough, reform and reshape and beautify our soul, bringing the kingdom of the heavens—the kingdom of God—inside of us. We see that as well in the parable of Christ: *"The kingdom of heaven is like leaven, which a woman took and hid in three measures of meal until it was all leavened."* (Mt 13:33) And our yearning for the presence of Christ that springs up inside our souls is expressed with these words alone—through this prayer: Lord Jesus Christ, have mercy on me.

It is difficult for us to understand the need for prayer, because it is difficult to know who we are. Most of us believe that we are perfect, without of course our being able to explain what perfection is. Perfection is simply what we are. We can't— or we don't want to—ask ourselves if it might be possible for there to be someone better than us, with whatever meaning we want to give to the word "better". We don't realize that inside of us we have confusion. In such a state, prayer can't happen.

'I am praying' means 'I am begging'—prayer means being a beggar. But what are we begging for? After all, we are perfect; we are "filled" (Lk 6:25) with virtue, with intelligence, with power. In order to pray, we have to stand before God as we are, not as we think we are.

Many times during prayer, some of those who manage to understand and to accept that they have imperfections have malaise and sadness inside of them. That happens because, with self-concentration, their attention moves away from the hallucinations that daze and delude the mind. Then they can see their soul as it is—sick and ugly.

They would have to have the strength to endure the horrible, painful view of their soul and to grieve—only that would allow them to continue their prayer. Otherwise they would turn to something else. But whatever else they did, they would still have the wound of their soul as a constant companion, without being conscious that that wound could lead them to catastrophe.

At the time of prayer (or rather that which we take for prayer) in our cell, the following situation also happens to many: through methods of self-concentration (prayer rope, regulation of breathing, etc.) we happen upon some kind of spiritual tranquility, saying words of prayer, like "Lord Jesus

Christ, have mercy on me." That proves that this tranquility is artificial, because it is attained when we have not understood the need for prayer—when we are praying mechanically.

That's why it is superficial tranquility. It is not due to the easing of our conscience. It is not the consequence of our monitoring of, and our mastery of, our passions. It is not the deep and undisturbed peace of our spirit that Christ gives us.

That becomes apparent from our behavior even immediately after the end of the "prayer". That artificial tranquility deceives us and makes us believe that we have reached a lofty spirituality—that we are virtuous. However it is not those who say "Lord, Lord" during the hour of prayer who experience the kingdom of God and the peace of Christ, but those who do the will of God—those who are the way Christ wants them to be. *"Not everyone who says to Me, 'Lord, Lord,' shall enter the kingdom of heaven, but the one who does the will of My Father in the heavens,"* Christ tells us. (Mt 7:21)

I think that artificial tranquility must resemble the condition that followers of some religions create within themselves in an egotistical way.

We also show our inability to understand the need for prayer during the celebration of a wedding. We are not aware that the performance of a wedding is prayer. The newlyweds and the guests show that the blessing of God is not enough for them, or rather that they don't need it for their good journey in life. That's why they seek the help of…rice!

What significance does rice have at a time of prayer? The throwing of rice during the performance of the wedding ceremony even reduces some clergy to using the holy book of the Gospel as a shield to protect their head from the rice that falls on it…

Those of us who decide to live as monastics also come from this ecclesiastical and familial "atmosphere". That's why, except for the few who are able to grasp the meaning of the Gospel, we don't know what it is that we are going off to do.

Many of us show by our behavior that we believe that the meaning of the prayers we read in church doesn't concern us. It's as if those prayers haven't been written for us, only for others. Our presence in church is a formality.

How many of us, at the time we are saying prayers, like the ones that follow, believe that we are talking to God about ourselves? *"I have become naked of virtues and have clothed myself in evil, and behold, I am veiled in shame. Jesus, lover of mankind, gladden me with divine adornment;"*[4] and, *"All-Holy Trinity, have mercy upon us. Lord cleanse us from our sins, Master pardon our*

---

[4] From the Parakletike Canon (The Great Octoechos), Tone 4, Tuesday Matins, Ode Four. —*Trans.*

iniquities. Holy One visit and heal our infirmities for Thy name's sake."

How many of us are there who, when we say the words *"heal our infirmities"*, believe that we have infirmities—spiritual weaknesses? From which infirmities do we supplicate God to heal us?

Throughout the length of the Services we continuously say *"Lord, have mercy."* How many of us, even once on hearing *"Lord, have mercy"*, see inside of us the need for the Lord to have mercy on us?

During the Divine Liturgy, we chant: *"We have seen the true light, we have received the heavenly spirit...."* Many, such as St. Anthony, saw the true light—the light of Christ. How many of us who say, *"we have seen the true light"*, can confirm that we have seen that light? How many of us are perfect, so that we can accept into our spirits the true light and receive the heavenly spirit?

I know some people about whom I can't be sure if they have seen the true light. But I see that they say *"Lord, have mercy"* with their hearts. They have found the road that leads to perfection.

We need the right conditions for prayer. To keep our mind (*nous*) in uninterrupted prayer for as long as we can, we have need of solitude and quietude (*hesychia*). There is also fasting to help us be like we should be at the time of prayer—which is the reason we fast. And our obedience to our abbot ensures our undistracted prayer. Without obedience to the instructions of the abbot, we can't understand the need for prayer, and we can't pray for real.

IV

You are praying, or rather trying to pray....You ask yourself: Who is it that I want to speak to, and what is he like? You seek him out with your imagination.

He must be majestic, you say, since he's God. Your imagination can't grasp anything majestic within you. Your attempt creates a disturbance within you. What is majestic in essence cannot be conceived by the imagination. You say: Christ can't be like what I see inside of me. Yes, but what is he like?

He's sad. You hear him say: My soul is so sad, that I'm in danger of dying. *"My soul is exceedingly sorrowful, even unto death...."* (Mt 26:38) Sad...Why? And so much, even to death....You think, you try to comprehend what His sorrow is like—to understand what He is experiencing in His sorrow. You see that you can't. His sorrow, impossibly heavy for you, must be majestic, since everything about God is majestic. Majestic sorrow....How can I see it?

You can't understand how sorrowful God is even when you see His sorrow in His human form. The sorrow of Christ must be as majestic as His light—His light that He showed at His Transfiguration. How would it be possible for you to face that sorrow, that majestic sorrowful light...?

You understand that God wants you to perceive His sadness. The Sorrowful One says: Since you can't see the magnificence of my omnipotence, I am sorrowful unto death. If you want, see the humility of my sadness. And you will understand that it is not weakness—it is grandeur, because I am sorry for you.

I am sad because you can't perceive that you are pitiful. If you weren't pitiful, what reason would I have to be sad? I become the way you should be—sorrowful—so that you can see me. Like always attracts like[5]....

If you want to see me, don't try to see me as the majestic God— you can't. You can only see me sorrowful. I will remain sad until you come to stay with me, *"in Me"*—until your heart is purified.

Try and understand what my sorrow is like, that sorrow that makes me sorrowful even unto death. Then you will also be able to grasp the beauty of my joy—the joy I will have when I see that you can know me.

---

[5] «Ὅμοιος ομοίω αεί πελάζει», "Like always attracts like", is a Greek idiom that comes from Agathon's reply to Phaedrus in Plato's *Symposium*. —*Trans.*

V

TIMON: If we all become perfect through prayer, then what is monasticism, and what is its significance?

THEOPISTUS: Monasticism is an expression of our love for Christ. Martyrdom—the tortured sacrifice of our bodies and our lives during the confession of our faith in Him—is also evidence of our love for Christ. Monasticism is a sacrifice of our souls, and of all of our other desires, for the satisfaction of our will to know the peace of Christ.

It is a consequence of the strong attraction of man to the perfection, the spiritual beauty, of the countenance of Christ. It is clear evidence of the need for the presence of Christ in our souls. Monasticism is our exclusive dedication to our cleansing, to our preparation for the reception of Christ into our spirit.

The life of Christ leads us to monasticism. Christ also lived as a monk; He dedicated time to the monastic life. Christ's forty days of asceticism in the wilderness, with fasting and prayer, is the form of monasticism. Those who decide to live as monastics are very far from the perfection of Christ. For that reason, they need more time than the forty days that Christ devoted to the wilderness; they need many years of asceticism to obtain the cleansing of their souls.

Christ practiced asceticism—lived as a monk—not to be healed of weaknesses, but to have complete and exclusive communion with God His Father. Christ lived monastically as One who is perfect. We live monastically as ones who are imperfect and infirm.

Not all people can become monks. Christ knows that. When the disciples of Christ told Him that for certain reasons it was in the interest of men to remain unmarried, He answered that only someone who sees that he has that power can remain unmarried: *"...He who is able to accept it, let him accept it."* (Mt. 19:12)

From the life of the Saints of the Church we know that God accepts monasticism. Saints like Saint Anthony, Saint Macarius, and others were monks, and they reached great heights of virtue and performed miracles. We see their wisdom in their words, which we read in the relevant writings.

TIMON: What is asceticism, Father? What is its purpose?

THEOPISTUS: Asceticism is the method we apply for the cleansing, for the healing, of our souls. Egotism is uncleanliness of the soul; asceticism, therefore, is our attempt, our struggle, to be delivered from egotism.

The "poor in spirit" and the "pure in heart" about which Christ speaks to us in His beatitudes are those who don't have egotism in their spirits. To uproot egotism from within us, we need a lot of effort, force, and asceticism. Christ points out our need for asceticism not only with His words, with His commandments, but also with His example in practice; Christ performed deeds of asceticism too!

Asceticism is physical and spiritual. Bodily asceticism is fasting, vigils, and inurement to hardships. Spiritual asceticism is obedience to a spiritual guide (to the abbot, for monks), as well as our effort to become aware of our imperfection with appropriate reasoning, such as self-censure and other things. Bodily asceticism doesn't benefit us if we don't practice spiritual asceticism.

Saint Anthony says: "Some have melted their bodies with asceticism, but because they lacked discretion, they were found to be far from God." Consequently, discretion—that is, self-knowledge and the perception of the will of God—is necessary. Those who don't understand that bodily asceticism is practiced in order to help us in the performance of spiritual asceticism, do not have discretion.

Those who have not perceived that the will of God—our becoming like Him—takes place with spiritual effort, with work that is completed inside our hearts, confine themselves to bodily asceticism. The purification of our hearts—which is the will of God—isn't accomplished with external efforts, but with prayer. A lack of discretion means, perhaps, that our longing for communion with Christ isn't great.

All those who want to relate to Christ practice asceticism, spiritual asceticism, precisely in order to do that which He says, and in order to be directed towards Him. Saint Basil practiced asceticism; Saint Anthony....

Christ suggests to us—He wants for us—to become perfect, and He tells us what we need to do to achieve perfection. That which we need to do—in accordance with the commandment of Christ—can only be characterized as asceticism. Christ tells us: To keep watch, in order to notice when He comes to us (Mt. 24:42); to keep watch and pay attention so that we don't find ourselves unprepared when we face our weaknesses and fall into temptation. (Mt. 26:41, Mark 13:33-37)

To understand that the gate we pass through in order to come to the place of virtue is narrow. The narrow gate connotes the great effort it is necessary for us to make, in order to be able to be like Christ wants us to be. *"Enter by the narrow gate...."* (Mt. 7:13)

To have patience, to persist in the efforts that we need to exert in order to be healed—in order to save our souls. (Lk 21:19) To be "violent". (Mt. 11:12) In order to win the kingdom of the heavens, to force ourselves—to strive hard.

To labor in order to progress in the performance of His will. (Mt. 25:14-30) To deny ourselves and our desires that are not in accordance with the will of God. To carry our cross; to desire to suffer every sorrow of our attempts to accomplish the performance of the will of God. (Mt. 16:24)

The words that Christ uses to define our task are: keep vigil (be watchful), pray, strive, narrow gate, patience, violent, labored, gained, let him deny himself, let him take up his cross; all those words and phrases mean asceticism. The taking up of our cross alone shows how great and painful the effort we have to exert is, in order to do the will of God—how difficult it is to sacrifice our own will.

The denial of ourselves is realized in the monastic life through the decision of the monk not to satisfy his desires, but always to obey the suggestions of his spiritual guide, the abbot. This obedience, this self-denial of ours, leads us to healing from the sickness of egotism and to the experience of spiritual rest which the performance of the will of God grants.

Christ says other words to us, with the meaning of asceticism as well: pull out, take the plank out of your eye.... (Mt. 7:5); ask, seek, knock. (Mt. 7:7)

To ask from Christ the way we should (in order for Christ to accept our petition) is also difficult; for that reason, we have to practice asceticism to become capable of asking from Christ— of asking like the tax collector of the parable (Lk 18:13), or like the disciple of Saint Anthony, Paul the Simple. The tax collector asked with awareness of his errors and with sorrow for his withdrawal from God. The monk Paul the Simple had such a relationship with Christ that he could demand of Him the fulfilment of his requests.

Once he was praying for Christ to heal a demoniac, but Christ didn't satisfy his request. Because of that, he climbed up on a rock when it was unbearably hot out and said to Christ: So you know, I'm not coming down from this rock if you don't heal this person. Christ immediately freed the demonized man from his torment.

Christ tells us that he came to save the person who is lost (Mt. 18:11), the person who has lost the health of his soul and his contact with God, because without Christ, man cannot do anything to save his diseased soul. If we have perceived that without Christ we can't do anything, we understand that it is necessary to ask for His help and His mercy. Because of that, asceticism requires that we always keep in our conscience the truth that without Christ we can't do anything.

Christ tells us that without Him, we cannot become perfect (*"...without Me you can do nothing"* (Jn. 15:5)), but He likewise asks us not to remain inactive, not to wait apathetically for him to heal us. He indicates to us that it is necessary for us to struggle spiritually, to force ourselves to become perfect—the way He wants us.

This violence to ourselves, this effort, is necessary because our spiritual weakness doesn't always allow us to ask Christ with all of our hearts. We seek Christ—His mercy—through prayer. Saint Gregory the Theologian says that we have as much need for prayer as we have of breathing.

Prayer is a difficult task for two reasons. First, if our soul is not pure, we have not been freed from our egotism, and when we pray it is not possible to see Christ, to Whom we are speaking. We address Christ, Who is unknown to us, and in Whom we believe with imperfect faith. We don't even know Him from the experience of His peace, which He gives to those who love Him.

Second, we don't even know ourselves. The weakness of our souls leads our mind (*nous*) to occupy itself with unhealthy spiritual investigations. As long as we don't see Christ, in order to want to seek Him, it is necessary to see ourselves as we are—to see the hell that we have inside our souls. The hour that we pray, if we are not aware of the fearsome catastrophe that our soul has experienced because of our egotism, our mind (*nous*) is not seized by the need for prayer, but occupies itself with unprofitable thoughts that weaken or cause our desire to seek Christ's mercy to vanish.

Effort, asceticism, is needed to cast out unprofitable thoughts from our minds (*nous*), and to turn our attention to the poor condition of our souls and to our spiritual emptiness, and to become aware of the need for prayer. Prayer is our most difficult task for exactly this reason—because it requires effort for us to understand the need for it.

Our subconscious turmoil, our callousness, our insensitivity, need to be transformed into grief in order for us to want to take refuge in prayer. Of course we are not talking about the prayer that we make reading prayer books, but about the prayer that springs forth spontaneously from the depths of our spiritual mourning, like the prayer of the tax collector of the parable, or of the thief who was crucified with Christ.

Christ knows that in order to heal our afflicted souls, it is necessary for us to become aware of our poor spiritual state; because of that, He also sets out for us, besides other things, those spiritual exercises that He indicated to Saint Anthony on the one hand, and to the Athonite Russian monk Silhouan on the other.

He suggested to Saint Anthony to consider that he was a sinner and that he would go to hell. Certainly Saint Anthony didn't find himself in such a spiritual condition that he would go to hell; thus he understood that it was necessary for him to practice this spiritual exercise that Christ indicated to him in order to be able to protect himself from onsets of egotism and to progress towards perfection. He was granted to consider that all people were good, and that only he was a sinner and would go to hell.

To the monk Silhouan, Christ suggested to keep his mind (*nous*) in Hades and to not despair. Silhouan was practiced in this exercise for many years and he reached a great height of spiritual perfection. His Church has canonized him as a Saint.

These spiritual exercises of Saint Anthony and Saint Silhouan were difficult feats of asceticism; our spirits require much effort and force to remain steadfast in the consciousness of the meaning of those exercises. Keeping our mind (*nous*) in Hades is the passage through the narrow gate and the difficult way about which Christ speaks to us. (Mt. 7:14) Whoever comes up against and fights with spiritual opposition, and with temptations—whoever knows the life of the spirit in all of its manifestations—understands the meaning and the need for spiritual asceticism.

Christ also points out to us the need for asceticism, for effort, with His own forty-day ascetic exercise in the wilderness. It is awe-inspiring and uniquely instructive for us to see that Christ—the Perfect One—practiced asceticism.

Christ knew that the devil would tempt Him, that he would try to put Him under his thumb and to separate Him from God, His Father. To fight against the devil and confront his temptations, Christ prepared with asceticism. Christ practiced his asceticism in the proper place and went into the wilderness for that purpose; Christ made the desert His place of ascetic labor.

Christ knows that in order for man to become perfect, it is necessary to confront the temptations of the devil. He likewise knows that man becomes aware of himself perfectly in solitude, in quietude (*hesychia*), and that in silence (*hesychia*) he is able to concentrate all of his spiritual powers in order to repel the attacks of the devil.

Christ experienced all of the spiritual conditions that we are compelled to become acquainted with. Through His life he becomes a model for us and He gives us the strength to win, just like He won. Christ did not fight His battle with the devil in the city, among other people. Only in the wilderness, alone, undistracted by different pursuits, with forty days of fasting and prayer—the Christ!—did He prepare to receive the personal attack of the devil.

Before Christ begins His work for our salvation, He practices asceticism for His personal completion! Christ began His preaching after His forty-day asceticism and His victory over the devil in the wilderness.

TIMON: Is prayer always a laborious task?

THEOPISTUS: The opinion of Fr. Agathonus (the contemporary of Saint Anthony), that prayer is the most difficult task, applies to us for prayer that doesn't spring up spontaneously from our souls—for prayer that takes place formally.

If we pray formally, our "prayer" is cut off from the desire for communion with God by strange thoughts. Any of us who faces this situation, if we want to persist in our "prayer", has to exert effort in order to cast out of our minds (*nous*) thoughts that interrupt our attention from the words of the prayer. That can't be considered prayer.

Saint Maximus the Confessor says that someone who loves God prays uninterruptedly. (*Philokalia*, vol. ii) For the person who prays uninterruptedly, from love for God, prayer is not a difficult task, because he is not impeded from his desire to commune with God by irrelevant thoughts. Someone who loves Christ with all his heart wants to have him continuously in his mind, just as we constantly want to have in our minds people whom we love especially.

Christ—with His words, 'Come to Me, all of you who are tired and disappointed from your pointless spiritual searches, and I will give you rest' (Mt. 11:28)—calls us to go to Him, to know Him, and to want Him to give us healing and rest for our souls. Our answer to this call of Christ's takes place chiefly through prayer.

Our journey towards Christ is a mystical and spiritual journey. It takes place with the preeminent spiritual means— prayer. Prayer expresses our desire to seek out Christ, our desire to receive him into our heart, into our spirit.

We don't go to Christ with different acts, with charitable works or with sermons of the word of God that we make as preachers, because we can do that even without having love in our hearts, as the Apostle Paul also tells us (1 Cor. 13:1-3). We go to Christ with our humility and our love, which we express through prayer.

We perform the first and great commandment, *"You shall love the Lord your God with all your heart, with all your soul, and with all your mind"* (Mt. 22:37-38), through prayer. From the words of this commandment, we see that our love for Christ reveals itself secretly inside us, within our heart, in our soul, and in our mind (*nous*).

Christ asks us to abide in Him, and He wants to abide in us, in order to bring much spiritual fruit into our souls, and so that we can become as He instructs us—humble, merciful, and peaceful. (Jn. 15:4-5) Our union with Christ is spiritual and takes place through the preeminent spiritual work, prayer. We abide in Christ with prayer. Prayer is the means that leads the perfect, the holy, to the vision of the uncreated light—the light of the face of Christ.

Christ doesn't only recommend that we pray—He prays too. The love of Christ for God His Father also expresses itself through prayer.

Because Christ loves His Father, he feels the need to commune, to speak with Him. For that reason, He prays to His Father, and He prays a lot. He prays because He wants to be alone with His Father, and to have His spirit directed exclusively toward Him, in order for His communion with Him to be perfect.

To be uninterrupted during the hour of His prayer, Christ ensures the proper conditions—solitude and quietude (*hesychia*). He goes up on the mountain (Mt. 14:23); he goes to a deserted place (Mk 1:35, Lk. 5:16). The prayer of Christ lasted many hours, and he prayed there, up on the mountain, all night long. (Lk 6:12)

Christ had prayer as His support even in His struggle to sacrifice His own will to the will of His heavenly Father, a little before the sacrifice of His life on the Cross. Christ's spiritual struggle to obey the will of His Father was so unbearably painful and exhausting that, to be strengthened, He prayed very insistently and fervently, while His sweat from the intensity of His struggle fell to the ground like thick clots of blood. (Lk 22:44)

VI

TIMON: The will of God is for us to become perfect, but also for us to love others. How do monks show their love inside the monastery, since they don't find themselves near anyone who needs their help? Isn't it egotistical for monks to live in a monastery and only take care of themselves?

THEOPISTUS: Not all the monks of a monastery have the capability of doing charitable works to show their love. For the provision of material help to others, the leaders take care of the monastery. However, as many of the monks who can, help others spiritually, discussing their different problems with them when they seek them out for that. They show their love in that way.

It's not egotistical for the monk to be occupied with becoming perfect, even without taking care of others; because it shows that he has the strength to acknowledge his imperfection and his weakness. He understands that he isn't better than others, thus he can help them. That's why he has as his work the gathering of his personality.

He understands that he can't become everyone's teacher—a missionary—if he himself doesn't become as God wants him to be. He doesn't deceive himself, believing that he has so much love as to be able to dedicate himself to the service of others. He is held together by the consciousness of his imperfection.

The conscientious monk decides to work for others when he can really have love as his motive. Then his offering doesn't become like cerebrally programmed "social work".

The will of Christ is for us to love others. He even tells it to us as a commandment. The question is, however, if we *can* love—if we have that capability. Likewise, we also need to know what the meaning of love is.

Christ knows that those who are capable of loving are few. To the others—to the many, to those who can't love—he gives the command for them to acquire the capability. Of course, with His commandment, Christ doesn't force us to obey Him. He allows us to be free to follow Him, if we want.

Through His commandment, He has the intention of making us understand how necessary it is for us to love, because He knows what love is for us. Love is the main, the most important component of the health of our soul. Love is the proof of our perfect, absolute spiritual health.

Christ wants us to be spiritually healthy. Because of that— and only because of that—he tells us to love. We love not for the good of others—not because there has to be someone to help those in need. We love for our own good, in order to be in our natural condition.

In the phrase "we must love others", our attention needs to be focused on the words "<u>we love</u>" and not on the word "<u>others</u>"—in order to see who we are, to see if we have the faculty of spiritual health, of love. And when we love, we are well not because we show our love to others, but because we have love inside our souls.

Speaking of love, even Oscar Wilde sees it, I think, as having that meaning that Christ gives it—for it to be that love that our soul needs in order to have its strength and its beauty.

Christ connects love with perfection. We see Him tell us in the Gospel that to become perfect we have to love everyone, even our enemies. (Mt 5:43-48) In order to be able to love truly, it is necessary for our soul to have been freed from every weakness; to not have the sickness of egotism—to be in its natural condition.

Only someone who loves perfectly can know joy in all of its splendor, but also descend into the bottomless darkness of sorrow. The one who loves has tranquility, rest, and freedom in his soul. Only someone who loves is free inside himself, and the horizon of his freedom is boundless.

Our love is perfect—that is, we are in our best condition—if we love Christ. Certainly God isn't in need of our love. We are in need of loving Him, in order for the beauty of the face of Christ not to remain unknown to us, so that we can see the powers of our soul develop to the height of the perfection of God.

In another place in the Gospel (Mt 25:34-40), Christ speaks in a way that could make us think that the reason we must love isn't for the attainment of our spiritual health, but for the benefit of others (e.g. the offering of food to the hungry). But Christ uses the simplest of proofs, those that are obvious, even when He is referring to our love, so that it can be understood by everyone.

He tells us that He will have us in His kingdom if we give food to the hungry, if we help those who are in need. But with these words of His, He wants to explain to us that we will be with Him because we love. To the one who could falsely claim that he also loved, Christ answers simply: It is not possible that you loved, since you didn't give bread to one who hungered and asked you for it, while you had even more than enough for yourself. Neither were you interested in seeing the one who was in prison.

Works of charity are proof of love, but not always though. For that reason, Christ likewise tells us that blessed are the merciful. He doesn't say the ones who show mercy: *"blessed are the merciful, for they shall receive mercy."* (Mt 5:7) That is, blessed are those who participate in the problems of others with their heart and not to show off. Of course those who give mercy are blessed if they are merciful.

Christ wants to make us understand that *how we are* has significance for us, not *what we do.* Our spiritual condition has significance, not our external work. In the Gospel according to Saint Matthew, in none of the "beatitudes" of Christ do we see reference being made to works of charity or to external works. All of those "beatitudes" refer to spiritual experiences.

Christ accepts those who love, whether they express their love with works, or whether they don't have the capability of doing works of charity. He knows when someone has loved, even when he has no external proof of his love, because He sees his soul. He sees in the heart of man his joy for the good of others and his sorrow for their misfortunes. That joy and that sorrow can show a more perfect love than the love of someone who expresses it with charitable works.

Even the Apostle Paul points out that our good works are not always proof of love. He tells us that even if we distribute all of our possessions for the good of others, without love we don't benefit at all: *"And though I bestow all my goods...but have not love, it profits me nothing."* (1 Cor. 13:3) It appears from here as well that our good external manifestations are not always proof of internal perfection. Love can also be invisible, secret. Even then it is accepted by God, Who—even if it is hidden—can see it.

Our love for God is mainly mystical. Only He can know it within the depths of our hearts. The person who loves God, who loves Christ, from the bottom of his heart, arrives at perfection. Love is light. Just as the light of the sun has different colors and breaks down into those, love encompasses all the virtues, all the components of health.

Someone who loves isn't satisfied only when he gives. He accepts with joy the gifts of those whom he loves and he considers them as precious. His greatest joy is to see the faces he loves and to let the beauty of their souls into his heart.

Love makes us gladly equate our will with the will of those we love—to willingly sacrifice our own desires for the preferences of others. And we show our love to God in sacrificing our own will for His will. Because we love Him, we want to keep His commandments. We say to Christ that which He says to His Father, Whom He loves: *"...and I will love him and manifest Myself to him."* (John 14:21) The person to whom Christ appears has reached the highest degree of perfection; he has accomplished the aim of life.

The chief characteristic of love is not our disposition to help those who are in need; it is the respect we have in the depths of our heart for others, for everyone. If we have the power to love, others—all—are precious persons for us. We approach them with infinitely greater care than that which the poet Nicephorus Vrettakos[6] has for flowers.

---

[6] Nicephoros Vrettakos (1912-1991) is widely considered to be one of modern Greece's most important poets. —*Trans.*

The poet writes in one of his poems (if I remember his words precisely): *"I washed and washed again my hands to caress a flower...."* I imagine how Nicephorus would have prepared himself to caress the smile of a child with his gaze.

A friend of mine asked a mutual acquaintance of ours—a teacher—to help his child with his school lessons. His child did not like school. Because of that, the teacher did what he could to make his company with the child so pleasant that he would comfortably pay attention to whatever he taught him. He gave the child games and sweets, which he accepted, expressing his pleasure.

One day, the child had the following conversation with the teacher. The child began:

— Gregory, I understand that you love me.

— How do you understand that I love you, my Taki?

— I understand it because you speak to me nicely, and you respect me.

The teacher told me that this answer of the child's amazed him. The child didn't consider the offer of the sweets and games that he accepted from the teacher as proof of love. He saw love in the respect. He didn't refer to other words that demonstrate love. He didn't say, you take care of me, or you pay attention to me. He said, you respect me.

While love is health, hate is sickness. We see the symptoms of spiritual sickness in the soul of someone who hates. We see agitation and confusion. We see the hardening and inflexibility of neurosis.

He who hates can't rejoice. He can sing and he can laugh, but he can't be happy. He suffers without even realizing it.

Just as not all other people are perfect, we monks are not all perfect either. Therefore not all of us monks have the power to love. I don't know how many of us there are who believe that we love. Our residence in the monastery is justified if we try, if we practice making ourselves capable of somehow grasping the meaning of love. When we have achieved that, it means that we have also made a beginning in the improvement of the health of our soul.

There are cases in which love manifests itself in our preference to accept from others whatever they give us, rather than giving them what we want. Love discerns when we should give, and when we should receive. Luke the Evangelist refers in his Gospel (Lk 9:38-42) to the way in which the sisters, Martha and Maria, each showed their love to Christ when they welcomed Him into their house.

Martha occupied herself with preparations in order to entertain Christ. She showed her love with the desire to offer, to give. She didn't want to remain together with Christ, to listen to Him speak. She saw what she would have given as having greater worth than what Christ was giving. She considered that Christ had need of her services, her hospitality, whereas she didn't need to learn what He was saying.

She believed that Christ was the Son of God, Who had come into the world. It seems, however, that she didn't have the lofty spirituality that would have allowed her to grasp that which Christ came to give us. Her love was not perfect. Elements of egotism appeared in her behavior towards Christ.

She didn't speak to Him with the necessary reverence. She asked him to tell her sister to stop listening to Him in order to help her with the work she was doing. Martha shows by this behavior of hers that her readiness to offer something does not emanate from pure love. She thinks that she loved.

Many of us—not only Martha—don't have the capability of comprehending what the motives of our actions are. Martha's readiness to offer something isn't capable of giving her soul true pleasure and comfort, since it is obvious that there is egotism in her motive. She offers, but not out of love. Christ points out to her that she is occupying herself with work that doesn't benefit her, while her sister, Maria, chose to do that which was good for her.

Maria showed her love for Christ by her preference to receive what He was giving. She stayed near Him and listened to Him speak. She understood the value of the words of Christ. She saw that she needed Him. It wasn't satisfying for her to have Christ in her house and to not remain with Him to accept the honor the He was giving her by His presence.

Instead of giving, Maria received; she took from her Visitor, Christ. In that way, she showed her love. Her behavior towards Christ confirmed that she loved Him, because she stood before Him with respect.

Christ did not commend Martha for her eagerness to entertain Him. He praised Maria, who wanted to stay near Him to receive His teaching. Because He knows in whose heart there is love.

VII

TIMON: Father, have you known any perfect monks?

THEOPISTUS: I am not perfect, and because of that I can't comprehend the limits of perfection of the perfect. Even if I conversed with a perfect person, I couldn't understand him, since I don't have the experience of perfection. But I can say that I know conscientious, virtuous monks.

A monk acquaintance of mine showed his spirituality on the following occasion. He was passing by a place where a worker was trying to start up his chainsaw, without success. As soon as he saw the monk, he told him about it. He suggested to him: Make your (sign of the) cross and it will work.

The worker did as the monk told him. On his first try, the tool worked. The worker himself related that event to me. I don't know if the chainsaw would have worked at some point even without the worker making his cross; but I know that monk believed what he told him.

One day, as I was walking on the road on Mt. Athos, two young men passed by close to me. At that moment, one of them was saying: "He told me that a characteristic of humility is gratitude." What I heard seemed so important to me that I wondered who might have said it.

Immediately I thought: Paisius must have said it. I wanted to be certain. The two young men had gone some distance. I sped up my pace, and approached them and asked:

—"Excuse me, who told you that about humility, that you mentioned a little while ago?"

—"Father Paisius," was their answer.

I was amazed, because I believed that word of Paisius revealed a mental capacity of penetrating into the depths of the spirit and of analyzing its manifestations. I saw that an almost illiterate monk could analyze the soul and know the details of its spiritual life.

I could refer to some characteristics of humility, known to everyone else, but it would not have been possible for me to consider gratitude as one of its characteristics. Out of curiosity, I even asked others. No one referred to gratitude.

I understood the significance of Paisius's opinion intellectually, logically. However his word was not the result of a thought process; it wasn't the conclusion of deductive reasoning. It was the expression of his spiritual experiences. Paisius revealed the gratitude that he had in God.

But it was another monk—Aitherius—who made me understand that when I spoke to him about what Paisius had said. Aitherius, after he listened to me, remained thoughtful for a little while and then told me: "Paisius has experience...." And I thought, without saying it to him, that he, Aitherius, had experience, too. Otherwise he wouldn't have been able to perceive how Paisius had revealed his spirituality with his words. Aitherius showed that he too accepted the gifts of Christ with gratitude.

I related this story to my friend, Monk Evlogius, as well. When he heard it, I saw that he was pensive. He said to me: "I wonder what gratitude is like? What is the form of a soul that is grateful?" And he slowly walked away.

I'll tell you now about Elpidius. That monk had gone from his monastery to a city. One Sunday morning he went to church there at some monastery. After the Divine Liturgy, several of the faithful approached him and, full of enthusiasm, told him how they had decided, along with some others, to go to a cinematographer who had produced a work that falsified the life of Christ, and to protest, demanding that he stop showing the film.

They asked for Elpidius's opinion, and he told them: "I see that you are saddened by this film being shown. When you go to the cinematographer to protest, can you cry from your sorrow?" They answered that they couldn't cry. Then Elpidius told them: "Since you can't cry from your sadness, I think that your protest doesn't make sense." After that, those people abandoned their intention.

Eusebius is a monk, not a hieromonk. When I went to his monastery to visit him, he was very sad. I asked him what had happened, and he told me:

"An hour ago, a monk friend of mine (he didn't tell me his name) came to see me. He mentioned to me that he was tormented by a passion, which made it necessary for him to perform a forbidden action—a sin—every day. He has confessed that sin of his to many spiritual fathers, but he can't stop it. I'm very sad about his situation. When he confessed it to me, I listened to him and couldn't even say one word to him. I listened to him and cried."

After some time, I met up with Eusebius again. He told me that that monk had stopped committing that sin ever since the day he had spoken with him.

Now another friend from our group, Pavlos, spoke up.

PAVLOS:　　Father, you said that the monks confess to the abbot. Is there a reason for monks to confess?

THEOPISTUS:　Monks examine themselves to know if they are like Christ wants us to be. During their spiritual journey, by reason of human imperfection, they can make mistakes and commit sins. They confess those errors and all of their doubts, as well as their sins, to the abbot in order to get his advice and to get help in their efforts.

PAVLOS: Can we say that confession is like the
psychoanalysis that is done in psychiatry?

THEOPISTUS: The confession of Christians is psychotherapy—a
spiritual presentation—but a different kind of psychoanalysis
from the psychoanalysis defined by psychiatry.

Real confession is the confession of conscientious Christians.
That is the mystery of repentance and confession. The
confession of nominal Christians is not canonical, it is a
formality. We can understand the difference between
confession and psychoanalysis only if we compare the real
confession of conscientious Christians with psychoanalysis.

Confession is the spiritual act of a healthy person. The
conscientious Christian can't be spiritually sick. The goal of his
confession isn't the healing of spiritual maladies. He might face
various sorrows and dilemmas, and reach the limits of
desperation, but provided that in the depths of his soul he
remains inseparable from God, none of that will harm him. He
will remain spiritually healthy.

Before confession, repentance for some sin has certainly
already taken place. Without repentance, confession doesn't
have any meaning. Sin—visible or invisible—has disturbed the
relationship of the faithful person with Christ. It has caused
illness of the soul.

The conscientious Christian loves Christ and has personal
communion with Him, and because of that lives according to

His will. Whoever has not reached a high level of spirituality
and doesn't have perfect love may at some time, by reason of
his imperfection, lower his guard and sin—may distance
himself from God. His sin my confine itself inside his soul, and
not harm others.

The love that he has for Christ in the depths of his heart
makes him see the emptiness that has been created inside of
him by his moving away from Him. He is sorry, and he mourns
because of that. The grief of his repentance is real, vivifying.
He repents and mourns, not because he doesn't want to appear
as unruly through the transgression of some canon.

The moment that he repents, and the moment that he
confesses, the conscientious Christian is not focused on rules.
He is focused on Christ. He grieves because he has distanced
himself from Him. With his repentance, he beseeches Christ to
take him back close to Him and to give his soul His peace once
again. Like the Apostle Peter, he says to Him: Yes, Lord, You
know that I love you.

The process of repentance reveals the dynamism of the soul
of the penitent. He can know, monitor, and govern himself. His
soul's powers of resistance, with the fundamental virtue of
humility, effectively confront disease—sin. They neutralize it
with repentance.

Repentance heals the soul of the penitent, and brings him to
a higher degree of self-awareness, to a higher spirituality; it

leads him to the perfection of his personality. Repentance reveals that the soul of the person, while it has sinned and has become sick, hasn't died. Repentance springs from the person's love for Christ.

If the person didn't love Christ, he would not be aware of his separation from Him through the committing of sin. His repentance would confine itself to regret over some evil act of his, and would not come to completion with his desire to reunite with Christ. But then he would not be able to achieve perfect control of himself.

Someone who repents is spiritually healthy because he loves—loves Christ. Consequently, he loves his fellow man.

Through his repentance, the Christian is accepted by God, even if he does not have the capability of confessing. Christ called the Apostle Peter near Him without his having confessed. He called him, because He knew his repentance. He knew that Peter, despite his denial, held onto his love for Him in the depths of his soul. In the parable of the Prodigal Son, we see that the father accepts his repentant son before he has a chance to confess as he had intended.

The purpose of the mystery of confession, I think, is not the diagnosis of sin, nor the finding of the cause of the disturbance of the spiritual health of the one confessing. The conscientious Christian will already know that when he confesses, because he has the capacity for self-knowledge. He also knows the means of his cure from sin. He knows that in order to be healed, he has to seek refuge in the love of Christ.

The purpose of the confession of the conscientious Christian is the revelation and the confirmation of his love for Christ. That is seen as well from the dialogue of Christ with the Apostle Peter after the Resurrection. Christ is looking for Peter to confess. But to confess what? His sin, his denial? No. He is looking for Peter to confess whether he loves Him. Nothing else. *"Simon, son of Jonah, do you love me?"* And Peter answers: *"Yes, Lord, you know that I love you."* (John 21:16)

Christ, as all-knowing, knows Peter's sin. He likewise knows his repentance and his love. He doesn't ask Peter to confess his sin, because he knows that the confession of sinful acts does not always mean love for God. He asks him straight and to the point if within his soul there is that word that can keep him united with Him—love: *"Simon, son of Jonah, do you love me?"*

He wants to make Peter understand that he accepts him precisely because he loves Him, with such a steadfast love that he confirms it with his whole heart three times. Peter received forgiveness from Christ without His wanting him to confess his sin.

When asked by Christ if he loved Him, he didn't answer: Yes, Lord, I love you, but I denied you—forgive me. He simply said: "Yes, Lord, I love you." That said it all. His repentance was so deep, so drastic, that his love for Christ was firmly established in his whole heart. Christ didn't impose a penance on Peter for his sin, which was so great. After his confession of love, He accepted him right away.

In our confession we relate—as a rule—our external acts. We don't confess the cause that led us to those acts. But that cause, mainly, is the sin. That cause can ruin our soul even if it is not revealed, even if it doesn't manifest itself through some evil act. And that cause remaining hidden within us sickens and breaks down our soul.

The distancing of our spirit from Christ, the weakening of our love for Him—that is sin. That is the invisible cause that impels us to visible wicked acts.

The forgiveness of our sins is given by God, not because we have confessed, but because we have repented for our sins. We have need of confessing our sins and our repentance, because our spiritual father has to know the reason he is forgiving us, in order to be able to see how sincere our repentance is.

From the psychoanalysis that Christ performed on Peter, the difference between confession and the psychoanalysis that is performed in psychiatry seems clear. During psychoanalysis in the psychiatric clinic, a person presents the details of his sick soul and his cure is undertaken.

In the confession of the Christian, like the Apostle Peter, the health of his soul is revealed. He externalizes the preeminent component of spiritual health that he has within him—love. Of course he also confesses his sin, his infirmity, but the moment he relates it, he has already been healed from it by repentance.

The confessing Christian analyzes his healthy soul. The confession of the conscientious Christian is not a discussion to get an answer about uncertainties, nor to solve various problems.

Even Judas confessed, to the high priest and the priests. He confessed his act—his betrayal—and acknowledged that he had sinned. He regretted his sin. But the regret of Judas—his repentance—did not spring from his love for Christ. Judas wanted to be all right with respect to himself, not with respect to God.

He expected himself to be infallible. He understood that his betrayal was mistaken. Out of his egotism, he did not want to ask forgiveness from Christ. He wasn't sorry for his departure from Christ. He was angry because he made a mistake. He couldn't stand to see that he was wrong. Because of that, he gave his life that grievous end.

Nominal Christians don't seek to demonstrate love for Christ with their confession; they don't desire to have personal communion with Him. They look for goods from God, they don't look for God Himself. Just as they keep the other canons formally, they also confess formally, because they believe that for that reason they will be able to present themselves as perfect before God.

With this kind of nominal confession they remain spiritually stagnant; they don't make progress towards spiritual health. They don't have self-knowledge, and because of that they can't become conscious of the infirmity of their soul. They don't perceive that they need to heal the weaknesses of their soul.

They don't know the meaning of repentance, and because of that they confess not because they sense what kind of spiritual situation they find themselves in, but to appear in order through the keeping of formalities. It is possible for psychological problems to be present in nominal Christians.

Psychoanalysis isn't concerned with guiding man to God. The psychologically ill person who puts himself under psychoanalysis isn't pursuing the repair of his communion with God. He only seeks a cure from his illness.

He doesn't have self-knowledge and can't monitor the functioning of his soul. He can't take note of the cause of his situation. He has confusion inside him. He doesn't have inner strength[7], and he is not capable of finding his health again by himself, like the repentant Christian.

---

[7] Literally "self-strength". —*Trans.*

VIII

PAVLOS: Can we say that sin is a psychological illness?

THEOPISTUS: We see how psychiatry characterizes all those situations that the Church considers sin as psychological illnesses. Egotism, which is a psychological illness, is referred to by Christ in the New Testament as a sin, with the word pride. (Mk 7:22)

Christ characterizes sinners as sick and says that, for them, He is a Physician. He even refers to whatever relates to sin in medical terms. When the Pharisees express their opinion that Christ shouldn't keep company with sinful people, He answers that sinners are sick people and that He is approaching them as a Physician, in order to give them their health. (Mt 9:11-12)

In the book "The Ladder", Saint John Climacus[8] gives us among other things an analysis of a sin: insensitivity. (Talk 18) We see a description of a psychological illness—an analysis of the same sin, comparable to that of Saint John's—in the book of a psychiatrist, Pierre Janet, if I am not mistaken about his name. The similarity of the description of insensitivity in the

---

[8] Monk Macarius refers to him as 'Saint John the Sinite', but here we have used the appellation more commonly known in the West. He also labels the chapter of the Saint's writings to which he refers as a "Λόγος", or in this context "Talk", as opposed to what some English renderings of *The Ladder of Divine Ascent* call a "Step". —*Trans.*

two books is such that we can say that there is an identity of
spirit between the two writers—only the saintly writer lived
about one thousand four-hundred years before the
psychiatrist.

It is said that Carl Jung[9] studied that book, the "Ladder" of
Saint John. It is likewise said of that same psychiatrist that if he
knew that the patient who was visiting him was a Christian, he
advised him to seek his cure from his priest-confessor.

A psychiatrist I know told me that he noticed an
improvement in the situation of a patient when she confessed
to a priest. Certainly for there to be a full cure of a psychiatric
patient through confession, it means that person has come to
the place to be able to repent—that he has become a
conscientious Christian.

The priest-confessors who can somehow perceive the
situation of someone who has sinned, and can participate in
the drama of his soul, are few. We saw that a monk was so
touched by the confession of his friend that he cried. Most

---

[9] Carl Gustav Jung (1875-1961), a Swiss psychiatrist and psychotherapist, was one
of the most famous psychologists of the twentieth century and a founder of the
field of analytical psychology. He was instrumental in the development of the
concepts of extraversion and introversion, theories of archetypes and of the
collective unconscious, dream analysis, and many other significant contributions
to the fields of psychoanalysis. Jung, who believed that the human psyche was
inherently religious, was also known for his study of religions and even of the
occult. —*Trans.*

confessors endeavor to give a solution to the situation of someone who has sinned intellectually, with the formal application of the canons of the Church.

I don't know if, apart from descriptions of unhealthy situations, there are references in the psychiatric literature to the details of a healthy soul. But in the Gospel according to Matthew, with the beatitudes of Christ, we have an icon of the spiritual health of man. All of the beatitudes (Mt 5:3-10) refer to the characteristics of a healthy soul.

Even in the book "The Ladder" of Saint John the Sinite, we have an image of the spiritually healthy person. The Saint advises us: Become like a ruler in your heart, seated on high with humility. *"In your heart be like an emperor, seated high in humility."*[10] (Talk 7, 40) Surely, with those words of his, the Saint presents us—without meaning to—with an image of his own soul.

According to him, the spiritually healthy person is ruler of himself. He doesn't get carried away by his weaknesses, he neutralizes them. He has his mind (*nous*) seated in the highest place of his soul. From there he watches and monitors its workings, regulating all of its manifestations.

---

[10] Translation taken from: Climacus, John, *The Ladder of Divine Ascent*, from the series "The Classics of Western Spirituality", trans. Colm Luibheid and Norman Russell, Mahwah, NJ: Paulist Press, 1982, p. 140. —*Trans.*

He is not in danger of falling from that height, because he knows the limits of his capabilities and he is made secure by humility. That—humility—keeps him steadfast in his loftiness. From that height he must be able to see his spiritual horizon extend into infinity; and within that limitlessness to experience the comfort of freedom.

The philosophy and poetry of the ancient Greeks don't give us the perfect meaning of freedom. Neither can other philosophers and poets grasp its meaning up to today. Only the teachings of the Church can acquaint us with the meaning of freedom.

We see in the New Testament that Christ connects freedom with the knowledge of the truth. He tells us that only He reveals the truth to us, and that His truth sets us free. He sets us free, because He teaches us the way through which we will have a healthy soul, freed from everything that can weigh it down—that can bind it. He sets us free, because He makes us capable of having a free spirit.

Christ tells us clearly that since only He tells us the truth, we will be really free only if He sets us free. (John 8:32, 36) Christ likewise tells us that He doesn't simply tell us the truth, but that He is the truth, (John 14:6) because He is the Perfect One, and only that which He tells us is the absolute truth.

Certainly, whoever among us does not have a clean, healthy soul cannot grasp the soul's beauty, which is like what Saint

John allows us somewhat to understand intellectually. The illiterate monk Paisius also gives us an icon of the healthy soul, when, analyzing a certain one of its properties, the virtue of humility, he mentions one of its characteristic attributes—gratitude. And Paisius means the gratitude of people towards God.

The grateful person is spiritually healthy, and his spirit is clear. He can distinguish God clearly from his ego. He doesn't deify himself, and he doesn't reach out with his fantasy to places of perfection that don't exist for him—to God's "space".

When the grateful person finds himself in the places of God (such as when he prays), he finds himself in a natural place of reality. Gratitude makes the person steadfast in the security of humility and grants him the power of the perception of the truth. Certainly the grateful person also has the power to recognize the kindnesses he has received from people.

Christ also refers to our spiritual world with the word 'spirit', as it too appears in His first beatitude. This leads us to understand that the infirmity of our souls—psychological illness—is an illness of our spirit and of our character. It is, as the psychologist Karen Horney[11] says, a distortion of the character that has produced egotism (neurotic narcissism).

---

[11] Karen Horney (1885-1952) was a German psychologist and psychoanalyst, who developed a detailed theory of neurosis. She is often classified as a Neo-Freudian,

Egotism is not a disease of our reason, it is a disease of our spirit, of our character. Of course our reason is affected and disturbed by the poor condition of our spirit. The famous psychiatrist Pierre Janet[12] considered psychological illness as a disease of the spirit. What today we call psychotherapy, he called therapy of the spirit.

Through His "beatitudes", Christ shows us the course—the spiritual process—for the acquisition and foundation of our spiritual health. It becomes evident that the order of inscription, the arrangement, of the beatitudes in the text of the Gospel (Mt. 5:3-12) is not coincidental. In the first three beatitudes—to limit our reference to just those—the spiritual experiences which are suggested by those (humility, spiritual mourning, and meekness) are referred to in the natural (the psychiatric-scientific) sequence of their appearance in our souls.

Humility is referred to first (in the first beatitude, *"blessed are the poor in spirit, for theirs is the kingdom of the heavens"*), because

---

although she disagreed with Freud in certain fundamental respects. She is also considered by some to be the founder of 'Feminist Psychology'. —*Trans.*

[12] Pierre Marie Félix Janet (1859–1947) was a pioneering French psychologist, philosopher and psychotherapist in the field of dissociation and traumatic memory. He is considered by some to be one of the founding fathers of modern psychology. —*Trans.*

it is the basis of our spiritual[13] health. It is the power that lets us see ourselves as we are and relate to Christ.

Spiritual mourning is mentioned second (in the beatitude, *"blessed are those who mourn, for they shall be comforted"*), because it is the logical consequence of humility. Spiritual mourning shows that we have become fully aware of the reasons for humility, and that we have understood the significance of our remoteness from Christ. The humble Christian mourns, because he recognizes that he finds himself far from Christ, Whom he loves and towards Whom he wants to proceed.

Someone who doesn't want to have a relationship with Christ can be humble; however his humility is not part of his essence. It is simply rational, mechanical, originating only from the acceptance of his imperfection. That humble person can work at progressing in different areas, but he is indifferent about his spiritual progress. If he is saddened because of his imperfection, his sorrow will be unhealthy (depression)—it will not be spiritual mourning and it will not lead him to spiritual peace. It will not lead him to Christ.

---

[13] Monk Macarius refers here, as well as in other places throughout the text, to 'spiritual' health using two distinct terms—"πνευματικῆς", or 'spiritual', and "ψυχικῆς", or 'of the soul'. The use of these two separate terms incorporates the understanding of many of the Church Fathers that the human person is a tripartite being, with a mind (*nous*), a soul (*psyche*), and a spirit (*pnevma*). The limitations of the English language do not allow us to capture this nuanced distinction so easily in translation. —*Trans.*

Meekness is mentioned third, in the beatitude *"blessed are the meek, for they shall inherit the earth"*, because it is the natural consequence of spiritual mourning. Spiritual turmoil is what follows from the effects of egotism (hardness of heart, arrogance, and conceitedness). Spiritual mourning neutralizes our tendency towards egotism. It is incompatible with arrogance and conceit. Because of that, it preserves us steadfast from the turmoil that those passions create, and we can be meek and at peace.

The words of Christ are theology and sociology and psychiatry. Indeed, one place where we recognize the sociology of Christ is the episode with the Pharisees and the adulteress (John 8:3-11). We see there that, in order for us to have a correct opinion about social matters, we must first have a correct opinion about ourselves and know who we are.

In the same episode, Christ is also a psychologist. He knows that there can be no discussion with a person who is possessed by the confusion of hypocrisy. That's why he helps those He is speaking with to calm down. He doesn't answer their question immediately. He bends down and acts like He is writing with His finger on the ground[14].

---

[14] Blessed Augustine, in his *XXXIII Tractate* on the Gospel of John, says that Christ writes on the ground with his finger to show the Pharisees that he is indeed the

Waiting for Christ to answer, they calm down. They ask Him again. Now Christ answers them. The answer that he gives them could be considered to be chosen just for them. For that reason, in order not to anger them, he bends down again and writes on the ground without paying attention to them. Then they go calmly. The discussion with them has ended in the best way.

Now Christ converses with the woman, the adulteress. Although He has saved her life, he speaks as if He hasn't done anything more than anybody else. The answer that Christ gave to the Pharisees in this instance should be the rule for us each time we want to judge others.

Saint Moses the Ethiopian shows us how conscientious Christians behave in the spirit of the teachings of Christ. Once he was pressured by the monks of the *skete* where he lived as a monastic to take his place with others as a judge at a trial. They were going to judge a monk for some transgression.

He appeared at the court with a small bag slung across his chest and a large sack on his back. He was asked what those things meant. He answered that in the small bag was the error of the monk who was going to be judged, and he could see it. In the large sack were his own errors, which he couldn't see at

---

same God as He who wrote the commandments with his finger on the stone tablets given to Moses. —*Trans.*

the time of the trial, since they were behind him. The trial was cancelled.

The abbot of a monastery on Mount Athos was a good psychologist, without the relevant studies. He is no longer living. One day he received the visit of a foreign monk. The monk was upset and criticized his abbot. While he listened to him, he pretended to agree that the monk's abbot was wrong, and he asked him before leaving the next day to speak with him again. During their next meeting the monk was calm. The abbot made him understand that his judgments about his elder were mistaken. The monk accepted it and left quietly for his monastery.

As a psychiatrist, Christ is the perfect doctor. He knows the functioning of our soul completely—how its health is, its natural state, and what its illnesses are. Only He knows the means of curing the sick soul.

The therapy that Christ suggests to us is radical—it reaches the depths of our being. He tells us, for example, that we have to forgive others not with words but with our heart. Our forgiveness should be perfect, in order not to leave agitation in the depths of our heart which creates in us the desire to punish the other. The forgiveness we give should be perfect such that it gives our soul complete tranquility, total peace.

For our own good, Christ tells us to forgive from the depths of our heart, so that we have a healthy soul. The meaning of forgiveness is the attainment or the maintenance of the health of our soul.

Christ is a psychiatrist in his sermon on the mount, as well. In the first beatitude, *"blessed are the poor in spirit, for theirs is the kingdom of the heavens"* (Mt 5:3), He gives us the foundation of spiritual health. One who is poor in spirit is the antithesis of the egotist: the humble person. Egotism is a disease. Poverty of spirit—humility—is health.

Having an ego, which allows us to be aware of ourselves, to understand that we are persons different from the others, is natural; it's not corruption. Having an ego becomes a sickness when it is reduced to contempt of others—when it creates for us a false image of ourselves. That kind of egotism splits the unity of the powers of our soul and scatters those powers of ours away from us. It makes our soul like a split atom of matter. It makes us lose awareness of ourselves—turns us into lost personalities.

Our personhood, lost through egotism, is the <u>lost one</u>, the lost being that Christ wants to save (Mt 18:11)[15]. Egotism confuses our mind (*nous*) and does not allow us to understand

---

[15] The reference in the original Greek text is to Matthew 11:11; however, it seems that this is an erratum. The Greek word "απολωλός", as underlined in the original, actually appears in Matthew 18:11. —*Trans.*

the importance of the spirit. It deprives us of the comfort of the limitlessness of the spiritual life.

Christ wants us to fully understand the dynamism of the spirit. For that reason He tells us that *"blessed are the poor in spirit,"* and that we must know what <u>spirit</u> we should have. He says to His disciples: *"You do not know of what manner of <u>spirit</u> you are."* (Lk 9:55) Even Carl Jung emphasizes that the spirit has the most important significance for a human being.

The haughty person—he who is not poor of spirit—has confusion within his soul. He is high-minded, while spiritually he stands low. The high-minded person doesn't have the power to see his weakness.

The first-created opposed the will of God out of egotism. Their egotism made their love for God vanish from their souls and led them to cut off their communion with Him. They sinned even before they ate of the forbidden fruit. Their sin was the expulsion of love from within them.

The tasting of the fruit was the consequence and the proof of their lack of love and reverence for God. They didn't repent. If they had repented, they would have had the health of their souls. They told God the opposite of that which Christ said.

Christ said to God His Father: My Father, may it be what you want, not what I want. *"...not as I will, but as You will."* (Mt 26:39) The first-created said to God: It will be what we want, not what you want. But then they cast out from within them the grace, the gifts of God.

Now their souls were naked of the components of health—comfort, tranquility, and love. The first-created saw the nakedness of their souls, saw the emptiness within them, and tried to cover it up with other means—with "fig leaves"—with greed, and with hate; with those elements that kept them miserable. And thus began their hell—the torment of their souls.

That is what hell is. The emptiness that we have inside us, and the disappointment we experience when we try to cover that emptiness with elements that don't go together with the nature of our souls. And we also have hell inside of us when we consider that we are satisfied with those elements, without being able to perceive that we are missing something; when we are satiated, filled (Lk 6:25) with our enjoyments and with our imaginary perfection. Because then we close the path that leads us to the boundlessness of the spirit.

Through the prohibition of God, the first-created had the possibility of perfecting their self-awareness; of knowing the powers of their soul and acquiring the capability of monitoring and governing the contrasts that we have within us. If they had obeyed God out of love, their souls would have become more capable and would have ascended to a higher degree of spiritual perfection.

Later, after the interruption of the communion of the first-created with God, the relations between human beings were disturbed as well.

IX

Humility means the acceptance of reality. It is not possible to be aware of who you are, how strong and how weak, and to not be humble.

Poor in spirit doesn't mean someone who has little knowledge, nor someone who is unable to perceive and to judge. It means someone who—even if he is important—loves God and respects other people. Poor in spirit, humble, is someone who easily admits that his abilities—intellectual and physical—are limited and poor; someone who has a modest opinion of himself and a humble mentality, because he has clear knowledge of his strengths—because he has self-knowledge.

Poverty of spirit, humility, are health, because they are the faculty of a person to accept the truth about himself. The humble person admits that he has capabilities, and if he is a genius or someone talented, he accepts that too. But he isn't in danger of finding himself outside of reality—of losing his balance—because he likewise gladly accepts that there are capabilities that, while others have them, he doesn't.

The humble person avoids the confusion of the fantastical. He ensures his health, because he also turns his attention to his faults. Because he knows that those can ruin him, he examines them until he is free of them.

Man is not debased and is not diminished in his humility before God, because he stands in his natural position. The humble, conscientious Christian is not in danger of becoming sick with feelings of inferiority when he ascertains that he falls short in some area, because he doesn't seek to appear more important because of whatever it is. He gladly accepts whatever God gives him, and health makes his soul steadfast.

Like Saint John the Forerunner, he wants to decrease and for the gifts of God to increase within him; for his own will to yield, and for the desire to perform the will of Christ to increase in his soul. He also says: *"He must increase, but I must decrease."* (Jn. 3:30) Someone is humble when he accepts that without Christ he can't be well; when he understands the significance of the words of Christ: *"...without Me you can do nothing."* (Jn. 15:5)

Only the one who is all-powerful, perfect—the one who doesn't have anyone else above him—is capable of humbling himself, because only he is up high. He can humble himself truly and essentially; humble himself not by performing some act—some task, which someone like him, but with lesser value than him, is obliged to perform—but humble himself by becoming alike in nature and in essence with another being who is lower than him.

The one who can humble himself in that way, without losing his own nature, nor any of his attributes, is God alone. Only God can humble himself, because only He is lofty. Just like everything about God is magnificent, even his humility is majestic. The humility of God is an expression of his power, of His love.

Man cannot humble himself, because he is lowly. There is Another Who is higher than him—God. Man cannot become lower than what he is, remaining in his natural spiritual state. Man is humiliated in essence when he loses his spiritual health; when, due to his egotism, he falls from his natural place into a state of unconsciousness and hallucination—of fantasy.

Humiliation for man means corruption, degeneracy, disorder, and the loss of his personhood. Humiliation is not majestic for man. What is majestic for him is humility. Man is humiliated when he is not humble.

Someone who is humble reaches the boundaries of perfection, not when he is humble because he sees his imperfections, but because he is humble the moment that he comprehends with awe the difference between his own perfection and the perfection of Christ—the difference between his own greatness and the greatness of Christ. Then his perfection turns into gratitude for God, his Creator.

X

PAVLOS: Our instincts are natural. Why do monks leave desires related to some of them unsatisfied?

THEOPISTUS: Monks know that our instincts are natural. We don't satisfy the desires that our instincts give rise to in us when they push us into harmful excesses.

It's natural for us to take food; however, if we desire to eat food that is especially tasty, we can injure our health. Monks restrict themselves to plain food. It is not necessary for one of our instincts, the sexual one, to function, in accordance with medical science. If then we don't satisfy the desire that instinct engenders in us, neither do our bodies suffer any damage, nor do we become psychologically ill.

Monks are not in danger of becoming psychologically ill because they voluntarily leave some of their desires unsatisfied, of their own free will. They don't have aversions. Monks don't make the mistake of considering the pleasures that our instincts occasion in us as ethically unacceptable or evil. They know that God gave us pleasure too, and for that reason it is good, and enjoying it is not a sin.

The evil begins when the importance of enjoying bodily pleasure is overstressed or made absolute. Then the situation departs from the realm of the natural, because the person confines his soul inside the asphyxiatingly tight limits of some desire, without wanting to know the comfort of the spirit as well.

Monks know that as much as they can avoid anything is all well and good. They avoid it, however, to give themselves over undistractedly to their work. Otherwise, for someone to avoid something harmful and unseemly is self-evident and can't be seen as an accomplishment or a sacrifice.

The same limits that monks impose on themselves, others also apply when they are doing some job that requires us to have our bodies in especially good condition. Athletes do that as well, especially during a period of intensive preparation for competitions. I know a man who broke off his relationship with his partner in order to be able to dedicate himself to some scientific study.

If avoiding the satisfaction of certain desires is necessary for others to achieve their work, it applies much more to the work of the monk. Prayer, the work of the monk, requires perfect spiritual self-concentration—a difficult thing. At the time of prayer, a monk tries to be undistracted by any disturbance that can tear his attention away from it.

For that reason, he tries to have his body in the best possible condition as well, so that not even that creates impediments to his prayer. He avoids overeating as well as the satisfaction of every other unnecessary desire, with the point being for all of his attention, all of his powers, to be focused on his principal occupation—prayer.

Of course it is difficult to resist the demands of our instincts, since they are natural and spontaneous. That's why before anyone becomes a monk, he tests himself to determine whether he can submit to every kind of ascetic practice that the monastic life demands.

XI

PAVLOS: How can we have self-knowledge, to know exactly who we are?

THEOPISTUS: We only know ourselves when we want to accept God—Christ. Then we pray to Him. Since we are directed towards Christ through prayer, our mind (*nous*) becomes clean and we can see within us— we can have the perfect view of our soul.

To cleanse our mind (*nous*) and open its horizon towards the infinite, we need many years. Because effort is required for weaknesses and passions to retreat from our soul and for us to acquire the strength and the will to accept ourselves as we are. That's why Christ tells us that we have need for patience in our effort to know and to heal our souls.

Most people believe that we are perfect—that all of our thoughts are correct. Whatever enters our minds, we consider logical and nice, even when it's not, because we don't want to think that we could be making a mistake. In our opinion that we are perfect, we don't end up with correct, logical reasoning.

Our faith, that we are perfect, is perfectly arbitrary. A "voice", a belief, a conviction exists within us that makes us believe we are perfect the way we are. That has consequences that are unpleasant and many times painful both for us and for others.

Self-knowledge means a clear, tangible perception of our capabilities and our weaknesses. The way most people are, not only are we not aware of our weaknesses, but we even distort our virtues. We don't see them in their actual dimensions—we magnify them and in the end we make them useless.

In this condition, in order to acquire self-knowledge, we have to start by pinpointing our weaknesses, our mistakes. One mistake of ours with disagreeable results can move us and reveal to us who we really are. We have to want to remember that mistake of ours in order not to lose a clear picture of ourselves. We have to perceive the significance and the intensity of our strengths, and be aware of the limits of our greatness, in order to ensure our balance.

PAVLOS:　　Father, you refer to our weakness, but at the same time you say that we have greatness. Do you believe that man has greatness?

THEOPISTUS:　I believe that, because I see it. I know magnificent people.

God created man and gave him the capability of becoming like Him. The person who becomes like God, becomes great, since God is great. When Christ tells us that we should be perfect, He means that He wants us to be great. Because if the perfect person is not great, who can be great?

The greatness of man is not made manifest through the capabilities of his brain, but with the nobility of his spirit. Man's will to accept others, to respect them, to love them, makes him great. Love makes the soul of man luminous and gives its form a magnificent beauty.

Greatness appears in the form of the elderly, but also in the form of children. I remember the impression the magnificence of the face of a child made on a friend of mine, the moment that he declared his love for his mother when she had returned from some trip.

Her child, ten years old, showed his impatience to see her come. The mother came. The child showed his pleasure at her arrival in such a way that his face remained in my friend's memory of as one of the most exceptionally beautiful things he had ever known.

As soon as the mother sat down, the child went and stood in front of her, and he touched her with his body. He told her how he was while she was gone. The expression on his face was magnificence in itself—his tender gaze, his bright and sweet smile, the warmth of his voice showed the nobility and the courtesy of his soul. The child demonstrated that at that moment, his mother was the whole world for him. He wanted to show her that he was saving infinite beauty for her inside his heart.

She didn't pay any attention to him—didn't even speak to him. Maybe because she was tired, as she sat she stared fixedly in front of her. But the child continued to speak to her and to experience the most noble beauty inside his soul—that beauty which made his face so expressively beautiful, so magnificent, that my friend wanted to remember it always.

He likewise also wants to remember the amazing expression on the face of the child's father. The father saw the face of his child, and received the beauty that he was experiencing into his own soul.

He had fixed his gaze on the face of his child. That gaze of his and his smile illumined his face and revealed the warmth of his affection and his wonder at the magnificence of his child. The father showed that he took and placed the serenity of childhood grandeur into his heart.

As my friend tells me, that child loves his mother so much that he doesn't put her out of his soul, even if she treats him badly. The child is at a loss as to his mother's behavior towards him, and sometimes asks my friend:

—Gregory, what did I do to Mama for her to speak to me badly?

Without a doubt, that mother loves her child. Perhaps she speaks badly to him because she believes that is the proper way of raising children. It escapes her, however, that the souls of children are formed normally when the love of their parents is manifested to them with the requisite respect, and not with authoritarianism.

I know another mother. When I had gone to her house one time, I heard her say to her child, who was four years old:

—Johnny, <u>please</u> bring me that book.

Her child always willingly does whatever she asks.

PAVLOS: Father, you said that, in his sermon on the mount, Christ gives mourning as a characteristic of spiritual health as well. I can understand joy as health, but not mourning.

THEOPISTUS: There are reasons for mourning. Some people can't understand them, and because of that they don't mourn. Those who mourn are spiritually healthy, because their spirit is capable of seeing the reasons for mourning. They are not insensitive.

Of course it is natural for us to be sorry for the misfortune and for the pain of others. But mourning is a sign of spiritual health, mainly if it is the consequence of the awareness of our imperfections, our sinfulness, and our remoteness from God. We don't mourn, because we don't seek God.

Whoever seeks God mourns when they realize that they are far from Him. Their grief will bring them close to Him and then they will know joy; because Christ doesn't simply say that whoever mourns is blessed. He immediately says that they are blessed because they will be comforted—because their mourning will be followed by joy. They will have their joy when, through their mourning, they have become worthy of seeing Him: *"Blessed are those who mourn, for they shall be comforted."* (Mt 5:4)

Someone might say that whoever doesn't seek God is fine, since they don't have sorrow—since they don't mourn. But they are not fine. They think they are fine. They are—they appear to be—in good humor and take that good humor of theirs as joy. But their good humor is superficial.

If they could see into the depths of their hearts, they would realize that they are not comfortable. That's why monks go to a quiet place—to be free from the demands that impede them from seeing the depths of their souls. They want to be face to face with that depth and to explore it; and to beseech the kingdom of God to come there, into the depth of their hearts.

They know that Christ wants to bring His kingdom there, into our souls, because he tells us: The kingdom of God is inside you. *"For behold, the kingdom of God is within you."* (Lk 17:21) When they see that the kingdom of God is slow in coming into their hearts, those who are waiting for it mourn, and immersed in their grief, they continue to look for it....

For those who don't accept Christ, the reasons for mourning create an unhealthy sorrow, depression, hopelessness....They confuse true joy with enjoyment. They amuse themselves to be happy. Conscientious Christians rejoice even when they are amusing themselves.

Someone who is humble mourns, because he has the power to admit that there are reasons for mourning within him. He understands—to recall here a theatrical work—that mourning doesn't become only Electra[16]....

Mourning over our distance from God is dynamism, because it perfects our self-awareness. It brings tranquility, peace, and clarity to our souls, and encompasses within it the vigor of hope. If our souls, sick from passions, are not capable of knowing sorrow for their distance from God, it means that they are not capable of knowing joy.

Only when evening had fallen, covering the monastery's courtyard in deep shadows, did Fr. Theopistus finally stand up to go. But before leaving, he smiled at us warmly and left us with words that kindled a flame of longing inside of us. He said:

THEOPISTUS: It's late. In a little while we will retire to our cells. We will pray, and we will wait. We will wait to become worthy sometime of seeing—"in the middle of the night"[17] of our lives—the Bridegroom coming into our hearts....

---

[16] The figure of Electra, the mythical daughter of Agamemnon, has been the subject of numerous theatrical works from ancient through modern times. The specific allusion Monk Macarius makes is to a cycle of plays written in the early 1930s by American playwright Eugene O'Neill, called *Mourning Becomes Electra.* —*Trans.*

[17] From the *troparion* of the Bridegroom service (Matins of Holy and Great Monday), eighth tone. —*Trans.*

~ The End, and glory be to God! ~

Photo Credits and Acknowledgements

Front cover: A view of the porticos in the inner courtyard of the Holy Monastery of the Dormition of the Theotokos (Penteli, Attica, Greece), taken from the south entrance.—Photo by Lawrence D Robinson

Back cover: Detail from the front portion of the 'Great Schema' (also known as the 'Angelic Schema')—a special garment worn by Eastern Orthodox Christian monastics (both monks and nuns) who have achieved the highest level of monastic asceticism. The garment takes the form of a smock that is draped over the inner robes (in some traditions it also incorporates a hood and shoulder lappets), and beneath the outer robes. It is black, and is embroidered in red with the symbols of the Lord's Passion (the Cross, the spear, the sponge) and the skull of Adam, as well as various rubrics representing the 'Trisagion' (Thrice-Holy) prayers for the dead, and other liturgical mnemonics reminding the bearer that he or she is 'dead to the world'.

Special thanks is given to the most reverend Archimandrite, Father Loukás Zisimos, abbot of the Holy Monastery of the Life-giving Spring of the Theotokos on Poros island, Greece, for his generous permission to photograph an example of a typical *schema* garment.

www.ingramcontent.com/pod-product-compliance
Lightning Source LLC
Chambersburg PA
CBHW031518040426
42445CB00009B/294